the ANIMALS ROADSHOW

Desmond Morris
and the Roadshow team

To Ben.
With Best Wishes
19-12-91.

GUILD PUBLISHING LONDON

All photographs by Tom Howatt
with the exception of the following, courtesy of:
Richards of East Sussex, page 11,
Miss L. Pogodziski, pages 12 and 52 (left),
Jean-Paul Ferrero/ARDEA, pages 25 and 61,
P. Morris/ARDEA, page 26 and
Miriam Cardew, pages 31 and 32

First published 1988
Text copyright © 1988 by Desmond Morris
Main photography by Tom Howatt copyright © 1988 by BBC Television

This edition published 1988 by Guild Publishing by arrangement with
Jonathan Cape Ltd, 32 Bedford Square, London WC1B 3EL
BBC Books (a division of BBC Enterprises Ltd),
80 Wood Lane, London W12 0TT

Typeset by Ace Filmsetting Ltd, Frome, Somerset
Printed in Great Britain by
Redwood Web Offset, Trowbridge, Wilts

Contents

Introduction by Desmond Morris

The Animals Roadshow is, quite simply, a celebration of the animals with which we share our lives. As a television series it fills a space that has been vacant far too long. For years we have been able to enjoy superb wildlife programmes, but the tame animals with which we have formed such close bonds have been largely ignored. The Roadshow corrects this by concentrating on companion animals – our dogs, cats and horses, and the wide variety of different pet animals on which we lavish so much attention.

It is surprising that such a series has been absent from our screens for so long, for there are at least six million dogs and six million cats in British homes, as well as huge numbers of other pets ranging from the commonplace to the exotic. Despite this, by watching animal programmes on television in recent years the viewer has become more informed about lions and tigers than about dogs and cats. Perhaps it is their very familiarity that has caused our domestic pets to be ignored. What is there new to learn about something as well known as the family feline or the playful puppy? A great deal, is the answer. It is astonishing how little the average pet owner actually understands his or her companion. Familiarity may not breed contempt but it often does breed complacency.

Even those of us who have spent a lifetime studying animals have learnt a little more about them every time the Roadshow has set off for a new location. In each programme we visit a different town or city to investigate the local animal stories and to meet the local animal enthusiasts – people with a fascination, sometimes an obsession, for a particular kind of creature. Always we find the unexpected and uncover some extraordinary man–animal relationship.

The extent to which many such people allow their animals to dominate their whole existence has never ceased to amaze us. From the man with a lounge full of lizards to the murderer with a prison cell full of cage-birds, from the devoted ferret-fanciers to the specialists of the Tarantula Society, from the matron with a ward full of donkeys to the fish fanatic who contemplates his Koi carp for several hours every evening, and from the cat agony-aunt to the professional pedigree-pooch handler, they all show a dedication to their chosen species that is almost religious in its fervour.

The most appealing aspect of making the Animals Roadshow is that everyone we meet is pleasant, amusing and modest. This is no accident. People without animals in their lives often become egocentric, selfish and boringly consumed by the search for their 'real self'. Those who share their lives with animals are quite unable to suffer from such shortcomings – their animals will not allow it. They take people out of themselves. Their simple and uncomplicated trust brings out the best in their owners, men, women and children alike.

People who own companion animals on average also live longer than those who do not. Coming home from a stressful day at the office or factory, the animal owner is automatically soothed and calmed by friendly contact with a pet dog or cat. Blood pressure is reduced by the simple act of stroking a cat or patting a dog, and people with heart trouble gain significant benefits from having pets around the house. People with dogs enjoy the added advantage of having to take their animals for long walks. A brisk walk is by far the best form of exercise known to man – far better than jogging, whatever your more athletic acquaintances may tell you.

But the Animals Roadshow is not a do-gooder's programme setting out to tell you how to keep fit with pets, or a doomster's programme warning of the impending destruction of rare fauna, or a campaigner's programme about the many forms of animal cruelty and exploitation that still abound. All such programmes have their place on television, but because they insist on preaching to their viewers they are in danger of boring them and turning them away from the very subject they support – the animals themselves. The most attractive way of furthering the cause of animals, it has always seemed to me, is simply to show people how fascinating they are. The more we understand the subtle personality of a cat or appreciate the rewards that dogs have given to their human friends, the more likely we are to feel warmly towards them and the less inclined we will be to exploit them or treat them unfairly.

The message of the Animals Roadshow is therefore that animal companions are fun and also that the people with them are fun. It is a series full of shared smiles and is completely devoid of animal horrors. Because of this, we have once or twice been criticized for being too light-hearted and for concentrating too much on the pleasures of keeping animals, while ignoring the pains. I totally reject this criticism. There are too many horrors on television already and there is surely room for just one programme that shows nothing but people taking pleasure in their pursuits.

It has been a privilege for me to be part of the Roadshow and I have eagerly looked forward to every trip we have made. Because the people we have met have always been so entertaining and their animals so appealing, each location has felt more like a holiday visit than a business trip. This atmosphere has been immeasurably helped by the buoyant presence of my de-lightful co-presenter, Sarah Kennedy, by the tolerant leadership of our brilliant producer, David Martin, whose brainchild the series was, and by the untiring efforts of our two intrepid researchers, Polly Phillips and Fiona Couper.

There have, of course, been tricky moments. Working with animals this is inevitable. Blood has flowed on several occasions, but I am happy to say it has always been human blood. No animal has ever had to suffer in the cause of making our programmes. And where humans have suffered it has always been their own fault and not that of their animals. One reptile expert I was quizzing ended our interview with his hands dripping blood, slashed to ribbons by the needle-sharp claws of the huge iguana he had been holding. The reptile's fat body had hidden his injuries until he replaced it in its enclosure. Only then did I see the state of his hands and, horrified, asked him why he had not mentioned his problem to me earlier. He replied that he was so concerned with showing his much-loved giant lizard in a good light that he did not want to spoil the interview by interrupting it. Such are the people we have met on our travels.

Although no animal blood has flowed, certain other liquids have been much in evidence. It is difficult to keep a straight face when the impatient dog of the expert you are interviewing suddenly decides to ignore canine protocol and cocks its leg on her foot. And it is equally hard to keep up a running commentary when the dwarf pig you are holding becomes over-excited and relieves itself into your hands.

There is a nasty rumour that our revered

producer has assembled a secret tape of all these mishaps, including a lurid scene in which Sarah is savaged by a giant cockerel. But if he ever shows this tape we intend to retaliate by releasing a photograph of him crouching on all fours and howling up at the sky as he attempts to persuade a tiny toy dog to stare into the camera.

*

One of the difficulties in presenting a tele-vision series is that it is so ephemeral. There is no time to sit and mull over the individual items or the information they contain. For this a book is needed, and here it is. We have selected a wide range of interviews from those we have shown so far and have illustrated them with still photographs taken at the time. If you have enjoyed the Animals Roadshow the book will act, we hope, as an informative souvenir. If you have not seen the programmes, then the book will serve to introduce you to some of the most fascinating animals, and animal people, we have encountered. The world is full of such stories and we have only just begun to tap them. I have a feeling that the Animals Roadshow will be 'on the road' for many months to come.

The Dog with the Soul of a Monk

How would you react if a perfect stranger approached you as you were walking across the foyer of a hotel and performed a deep bow in the direction of your pet dog? This is what happened to Lhasa Apso breeder June Gamblin when she was on holiday recently on the Isle of Man. It was clear that the man was neither drunk nor joking. His actions were formal and serious, even solemn. So what was he doing?

To find the answer you have to turn the clock back to the time when the Lhasa palace in Tibet was occupied by the Dalai Lama, the spiritual leader of Tibetan Buddhism, known as the 'living Buddha'. Before he and his court were forced to flee into exile by the Chinese Communists in 1959, they were at the centre of a highly ritualistic religious culture in which dogs were believed to possess souls just like people. In fact, they recognized no difference between the

June Gamblin with a Lhasa Apso, one of the sacred dogs of Tibet

spiritual qualities of dog and man. Because of this it was accepted that the souls of departed monks could easily pass into the bodies of dogs and then, when the dogs eventually died, back into human bodies again. This faith in the concept of reincarnation meant that the monks in the Tibetan monasteries revered the dogs with which they lived. Indeed it became vital to keep special, favoured dogs around them so that these animals would be ready to receive the souls of the monks when the holy men died.

It was this role that the little long-haired dogs we now call Lhasa Apsos fulfilled, century after century, in the remote region of Tibet. The breed became so sacred to the monks that strenuous attempts were made to prevent them from travelling abroad. If, on special occasions, it became impossible to refuse the gift of a pair of Apsos to a visiting dignitary, the monks ensured that there would be no breeding from the pair by the brutal means of feeding the hapless animals powdered glass before they left on their long journey abroad. This meant that the Apsos soon died and their new owners put their misfortune down to the breed's inability to survive outside the high altitudes of Tibet. In this way the Lhasa Apso remained an almost entirely secret animal until very recent times.

The only exception to this in earlier days was the presentation of Apsos to the rulers of China. This occurred on a number of occasions, usually related to the repeated subjugation of Tibet by China. The Chinese Emperors were fascinated by the little, hairy 'Lion-dogs of Tibet' and instituted specialized breeding programmes of their own to produce a variety of 'Chinese Lion-dog'. At one stage there were nearly a hundred of these carefully-bred dogs in the royal palaces of China, and no fewer than eight distinct types had been developed by selective breeding. It is from these breeding programmes that the Chinese dog which today we call the Shih Tzu almost certainly arose.

The reason why these little dogs were referred to as 'Lion-dogs' is that the Tibetan Buddhists believed in the power of a supernatural spirit-lion on whose back, in legend, Buddha had been seen to ride. This lion was capable of reducing itself magically to the size

3

formed the foundation stock for a new pedigree breeding programme and within a few decades the Apso has risen to become one of the most popular small dogs in the Western world. In keeping with its curious history and its elevated role in Tibetan society, it has a strangely noble personality that has endeared it to all its recent owners. In addition it has proved to be a superb watchdog with amazingly acute hearing. This quality is something that has been developed over many centuries, since a secondary role of the Apsos in the great Lhasa palace was to listen for possible intruders and sound the alarm.

The problem the Apso faced if it did manage to surprise an intruder was that it was such a small dog that it could do little to apprehend the enemy. This difficulty was solved by providing the palace Apsos with terrifying partners in the shape of Tibetan Mastiffs. Frescoes have been found dating from as long ago as 322 B.C., showing the huge Mastiff alongside the tiny Apso. It was the Apso's barking that woke up the giant dog and stirred it into action, to savage the intruder and save the palace from attack.

So, to answer the question we posed at the beginning: why did a perfect stranger perform a deep bow to a Lhasa Apso in the foyer of a hotel on the Isle of Man? Investigation revealed that he was a refugee from Tibet who had been a monk in Lhasa before the Chinese had driven him out and he was astonished to see one of his sacred dogs again after many years. The reason he bowed, of course, was that he was honouring the soul of a brother monk that he assumed to be nestling inside the little, shaggy dog, reincarnated in the traditional way.

of a small dog – the lion-dog – and it followed that any small dog which had about it certain leonine qualities would have powerful symbolic significance. So it was that the early monks set about creating a lion-faced, long-maned dog – the breed which has come down to us as the Lhasa Apso. When the Chinese nobility later began modifying this breed they added a further symbolic feature in the form of a saddle-marking over the back to suggest the seat on which the Buddha had sat when his spirit-lion had taken him from place to place. This marking can still be seen today on many modern Apsos.

The Lhasa Apso did not become established in the West until the 1930s, when the thirteenth Dalai Lama was persuaded to relax the rules and export at least a few specimens. These

The Smallest Horse in the World

The tiniest horses in the world today originate from a ranch near Buenos Aires in Argentina. They are less than 28 inches in height and therefore smaller than several of the largest breeds of domestic dog. (The record height for a dog is 40½ inches.)

These midget horses, far too small and frail ever to be ridden, were developed by the Falabella family at the Recreo de Roca Ranch over a period of about a hundred years. The story is a strange one. Towards the end of the last century it appears that an Irishman named Newton owned a ranch and a water-mill in Argentina. There were many Indian raids at the time. Sometimes a whole ranch would be wiped out during one of these attacks, and the rancher's livestock would then be left to fend for itself. Newton noticed that the horses of murdered ranchers often came to his river to drink and one day he spotted an amazingly small animal, the smallest horse he had ever seen. He decided that if he could breed from it he could create the ideal pet for his little daughter, so he set out to catch it. He succeeded and the diminutive animal became the founder of what was later known as the Falabella breed.

Nobody knows for certain how the horse came to be so small, but local legend had it that a group of horses was once trapped down in a deep ravine where they became isolated for several hundred years, growing more and more stunted with each generation and surviving on a wretched diet of cactus plants. It is presumed that the murdered rancher somehow acquired one of these mini-horses and kept it as a pet or a curiosity.

This story was handed down – as were the descendants of the horse itself – to Newton's grandson, one of the Falabellas, who intensified the selective breeding to make the animals smaller still. To do this he is said to have imported some of the smallest Shetland ponies he could find and crossed them with the dwarf horses.

This account was told to a British enthusiast, Lady Rosamund Fisher, about ten years ago by Señor Falabella himself. But she has no way of verifying it because he has since died and there are no records available from the early days of the breed's history to help us unravel exactly what did happen. This is unfortunate because the whole Falabella history has been challenged recently by members of the Shetland Pony Stud Book Society. In their view the 'incredible shrinking horse' trapped in the wild and surviving on cactus is a romantic invention to give the breed a more exotic appeal. It is their opinion that no 'mini-horse' was involved at all in the creation of the Falabella and that the breed was fabricated entirely from unusually small specimens of Shetland pony imported

Desmond with Lady Fisher, some of her Falabellas and, to her left, a Shetland pony

into Argentina by the Falabella family. They claim that there is a letter in existence from Señor Falabella, written in 1971, in which he states clearly that the Falabella is only a modified Shetland.

Within the circle of Shetland pony specialists, the tiniest specimens, because they cannot be ridden, are looked upon as freaks and are discouraged. They are not used for breeding. It is felt that Señor Falabella merely took some of the runts that nobody else wanted and interbred these to create a reduced Shetland which he then glorified with the name of 'miniature horse'.

Lady Fisher, who is the British Director of the World-Wide Miniature Horse Association, does not agree. Whatever the truth about the 'little wild horse' at the end of the last century, she believes that the Falabella horses are not simply small Shetlands. She points out that their body shape is much more like that of larger horses and most unlike the stocky, short-legged, sturdy form of the typical small pony. The argument is a heated one and will doubtless remain unsettled until someone has visited the Falabella ranch and carried out detailed research into the history of these controversial little animals.

Whatever the truth of the matter, they are certainly remarkable equines. Their amazingly small size makes them ideal pets for anyone with a few acres in the countryside. They are described as docile, affectionate and intelligent, and with their spotted Appaloosa markings they are extremely decorative. However, because they are so rare they are extremely expensive, costing about ten times as much as a small Shetland. According to Lady Fisher, some unscrupulous dealers occasionally trick unwary customers into paying large sums for the smallest specimens of pure Shetland, passing them off as genuine Falabellas, and she told us that she herself has been duped in this way in the past.

The Shetland pony specialists deplore the promotion of the little Falabellas because they believe that their 'toy' appeal will attract fashionable people away from the pure, traditional Shetlands and may undermine the breeding programmes of these ancient equines whose ancestors were roaming the Shetland Islands as long ago as 500 B.C. There will clearly be a great

deal more lively debate on this subject in the years ahead but, having met the Falabellas in the flesh at Lady Fisher's country estate, we are bound to say that they do have enormous appeal as companion animals, even if to conservative pony-lovers they seem to be nothing more than stunted, unmountable freaks. There are many people today who simply do not have the suitable environment for riding, but who love horses and would like to own one as a pet. For them, whatever the traditionalists may say, the Falabellas are ideal and the arguments about their origins are of little consequence. A living rocking-horse is a living rocking-horse – and there can be very few children who could resist its charm.

The Biggest Dog in the World

The biggest dog that ever lived was a St Bernard rejoicing in the kennel name of Benedictine Schwartzwald Hof. He weighed in at 21 stone 11 pounds. Although this was an exceptional individual, all St Bernards are huge animals and it is this fact that makes nonsense of the enduring myth about this breed, namely that they were bred as specialized Alpine rescue dogs. What could be sillier than breeding a dog so heavy that it would be most likely to sink into the soft snow as it attempted to rescue a mountain traveller buried in an avalanche? Great weight would be the last thing that such a dog would need, but, despite this obvious flaw, the legend has persisted for generation after generation.

Part of the reason for the persistence of any myth is that it tells us something we want to hear. The image of a great, noble dog, trudging through a blizzard with a keg of brandy around its neck, searching out a buried body just before the last flickering light of life is extinguished, is so appealing that we are loth to let it go. So we ignore the impossibility of it and continue to enjoy the idea for its own sake.

The true story of the St Bernard is that, back in the days of Ancient Rome, armies crossing the Alps took with them their huge Mastiffs – the Molossian dogs – and some of these remained in the mountainous region that we now call Switzerland. They were used mainly as guard dogs in the mountain passes, and bred and lived there in this capacity for centuries. Then, about three hundred years ago, the monks of the Hospice of the Great St Bernard took in some of these animals and started to breed them as guard dogs for their monastery and hostel. Known at first simply as Hospice dogs, they had a secondary duty as guide dogs, to help the monks keep to the safer paths when they set out on journeys from their monastery. The dogs had a wonderful sense of direction and a good spatial memory, so that they could unerringly lead the monks along the safe routes, avoiding the deeper snow. In this role, of course, the great weight of the dogs was a positive advantage, rather than a disadvantage, because they would never risk going into deep, soft snow for fear of sinking down into it. As they were heavier than the monks, it was clear that where dogs could tread, angelic monks could follow.

If they ever did carry kegs of brandy around their necks it seems likely that the reviving drink was intended for the good monks rather than for desperate avalanche victims. Although less romantic, this interpretation does seem to have more of a ring of truth about it.

So, if the St Bernard was in reality a guard-and-guide dog rather than an heroic mountain rescue dog, how did the great myth begin? How have such impressive figures as 2,500 victims rescued in three hundred years been obtained? Or have they simply been invented? A possible explanation is given in an eye-witness report dating from about 120 years ago. The observer in question reported that some of the dogs had been trained to make regular daily trips to the

Jill Lux tells Sarah about her twelve St Bernards

resuscitation, then set off with the dogs to rescue the unfortunate victims of the icy environment. Perhaps these were the moments when the kegs of brandy came in handy?

This type of duty, along the known mountain pathways, seems most likely, the role of pathway guide, in special cases, involving a kind of rescue operation. Hence, no doubt, the start of the myth. And perhaps on exceptional days, when there had been an extremely severe storm or an avalanche, the monks and the dogs did go out together on desperate rescue missions. On such occasions, the dogs could use their incredibly heat-sensitive noses to detect whether there was a still-living body somewhere beneath the surface.

But these storm rescue operations cannot have been very frequent. We know, for instance, that in the year 1812 there was such an unusually bad snow storm that when the monks and the dogs attempted to carry out rescue work all the female dogs perished and the old line of St Bernard Hospice dogs came to an abrupt end. Female Newfoundlands had to be imported, and these were mated with the few surviving male St Bernards. The cross proved to be a disaster because the offsprings' coats were too long and collected so much snow that they too perished. Eventually more crossbreeding was carried out and a new St Bernard was created – the one we know today. So the modern St Bernard is not even the ancient dog of travellers' tales that worked the mountain passes for so many years, but a reconstituted animal of the last century.

Despite this, the modern breed is not to be scoffed at. It is a magnificent creature and those who devote their lives to breeding it, including Jill Lux, who owns no fewer than twelve of them, are happy to sing their praises. They may be huge and forever hungry, and they may drool and dribble, but they have, she says, the most attractive temperament of any breed of dog in existence. They are the essence of canine benevolence: calm, intelligent, reliable, sensible, affectionate and extremely peaceful. Altogether a dog with a personality that even his namesake, St Bernard himself, would have been proud to possess.

'cabins of refuge' constructed on the mountain pathways, for the assistance of travellers. The dogs set out each morning in pairs and if they found half-frozen travellers sheltering in the refuges they encouraged them to follow them back to the hostel, where they could be looked after by the monks. If they found travellers who were already incapable of moving, they returned by themselves to the hospice and, by their show of concern, alerted the monks to the problem. The holy men, armed with means of

The Cat that went Limp

Anyone who owns a typical cat will know the way it starts to struggle if it is held awkwardly. Its legs go tense and its body begins to twist as it attempts to right itself. This occurs because the cat has a highly-developed sense of equilibrium and cannot tolerate, even for a second, being off-balance.

Until recently everyone imagined that all cats, no matter what breed, would show this reaction. It seemed so basic to the feline character that a cat without it was inconceivable. But now the inconceivable is here, in the form of a remarkable new cat breed called, appropriately, the Ragdoll.

When you pick up a Ragdoll cat, however clumsily, it does not struggle or scrabble. It simply goes limp and floppy, as though it were a soft toy rather than a live animal. Some owners

Anne Ferguson with two of her Ragdoll cats

find this a most attractive quality, but others are made uneasy by it. The pro-Ragdoll people say it is marvellous to have a cat that is so peaceful and so totally relaxed in your arms. The anti-Ragdoll faction insist that it is almost 'creepy' to hold a cat that is so utterly passive and yielding. They feel that it is like touching a drugged animal – a kind of 'hippie-cat' that is so spaced out that it is beyond the reach of any normal relationship.

These differing opinions have led to a fairly sharp split between the supporters and critics of this startling new breed. The supporters want it to be recognized internationally as a valid pedigree breed for competitive cat shows. The critics want it kept out of all cat shows and preferably out of sight. They would be happiest to see it disappear altogether. The strength of their attack is due not merely to the feeling that it is an abnormal cat, but to what they see as the danger of that abnormality. They argue that a cat so extremely passive is incredibly vulnerable to abuse. The Ragdoll, they point out, is not only limp and floppy but also almost incapable of feeling pain or fear. So it would be impossible for it to signal to its owner that it was suffering or miserable. Young children could maul it about mercilessly. Any normal cat will only put up with so much grabbing and squeezing by infant hands before it screams or scratches and makes its discomfort known. The Ragdoll might literally be mauled to death by 'loving' arms without uttering so much as a miaow. It is cruel to allow such cats to exist, the critics argue, and the breed should never have been allowed to spread.

It began in a strange way, if we are to believe the official breed biography. Back in the mid-1960s, a farmer in California (an appropriate place for a hippie-cat to originate) owned a beautiful White Persian (or White Longhair) cat. One day, when she was pregnant, she was struck by a car and shortly afterwards gave birth to a litter of six kittens. The kittens all showed the floppy 'ragdoll' condition and it was immediately claimed that this was the result of the accident, which was supposed to have damaged their stomach muscles so that they could not tense up in the usual feline manner.

These kittens were bred with one another and then with Burmese and Birman cats. The result is a large, soft and exquisitely-marked cat that has an immediate appeal, even before its curious docility is discovered. But the strange feature of this story is that the floppiness, supposedly caused by the accident to the founding female, was inherited by the offspring of the original litter and is a genetic feature of the breed. Certain Ragdoll cat pioneers were foolish enough to suggest that it was the traumatic accident that had caused this genetic change but, viewed with cold objectivity, this is scientifically nonsensical. It has enhanced the myth

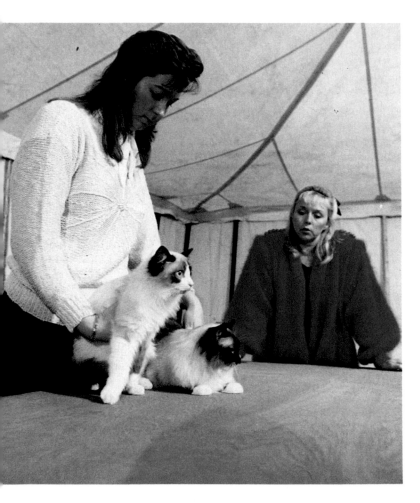

and mystery of the breed a great deal and added to its strange fascination, but it is no more than a figment of some fevered Californian imagination, strictly for Hollywood.

The truth about these cats is that, by some lucky (or unlucky) accident, they have inherited a character of extreme docility. All domestic cats are slightly more docile than wild cats. There has been a gradual genetic shift in this direction for about four thousand years, since the ancient Egyptians first began to control cat breeding. The most ferocious or suspi-

cious kittens from each generation were at a disadvantage. The quieter, more co-operative ones were favoured. But the process was never unduly accelerated by intensive selective breeding. Over most of their history, domestic cats were required to be rodent-controllers and as working animals they had to have their wits about them. Dopey cats that were too 'soft' in character would not have been all that popular. Nowadays, however, especially with pedigree show cats which only have to look perfect, there is a greater advantage in having a 'steady' personality. Cat show judges prefer to come out unscathed at the end of a long day.

The outcome of this shift in feline duty, from tough ratter to sleek beauty-queen, has been that greater tameness has been increasingly favoured. Before the advent of the Ragdoll cat the degree of docility was not, however, excessive. Then suddenly a line of cats arrived with, as it were, a double-dose of docility – some say too much for the cats' own good.

Seen in this way, the Ragdoll phenomenon is no more than the rather striking tail-end of a long process of domestication. The question remains, however, as to whether these super-tame cats should be allowed to spread and increase. Few have so far reached the British Isles, but we were able to meet some with the help of Ragdoll breeder – and defender – Anne Ferguson. She insists that they are an ideal breed for cat shows, since they raise no objections to the travel or the unfamiliar conditions in which they find themselves. And they are perfect for handling when being judged. Also, they are wonderful with dogs, never spitting at them or provoking trouble. In her opinion the criticisms are unjustified because these animals remain prize cats with a very expensive price-tag and are hardly likely to fall into cruel or casual hands. Providing Ragdoll breeders are responsible in disposing of their kittens and ensure that they go only to good homes where their special qualities will be respected, she feels there is no danger whatever in allowing the breed to increase. Indeed she believes it will become much more popular in the years ahead.

In her defence, it must be said that it is extremely rare to see other pedigree long-haired cats in careless hands, or wandering around as pathetic strays. The offspring of top show cats can nearly always look forward to a life of caring and luxury, compared with those of the ordinary crossbred moggie. So in the end it may be their very beauty that saves the Ragdolls from a life of mauling and misery, against which they would have no means of complaint.

The Hound that became a Sleuth

When the murderer of Martin Luther King, a man called James Earl Ray, escaped from prison in 1977, it was not a police helicopter but a pack of Bloodhounds that successfully tracked him down, a few days later, in the East Tennessee hills. This is the role in which we always imagine the Bloodhound at work, straining at the leash and eagerly sniffing the ground with its huge snout. But sleuthing was not the original function of this remarkable breed. Long before it was set on the trail of human scent, it was one of the most prized hunting dogs of the European nobility. Its first duty was to pursue not people, but deer.

Brought to Britain in the eleventh century by William the Conqueror, the Bloodhound was so favoured as a royal hunting companion that the new king brutally ordered that all other breeds of dogs on his lands must have three toes amputated so that they could not compete with the Bloodhounds in the hunt for game. Their very name reflected their high status. The prefix 'blood' was not meant to indicate that they were bloodthirsty. It was used in a completely different sense, indicating 'pedigree', as in 'blood royal' or 'blood horse'. So the Bloodhound was a 'pedigree hound' – a royal dog of noble birth.

The special value of this breed of dog during the staghunt was its ability to follow the scent of a wounded animal with great tenacity over amazingly long distances. It could follow a trail long after it was too 'cold' for other breeds, and it became the most valued scent dog in the country.

Its tracking abilities led in the Middle Ages to its being used after battles, to track down the fugitives from the ranks of the vanquished armies. As they fled into hiding, the Bloodhounds were set after them. This new function of man-hunting lasted for centuries, sometimes with spectacular results, such as the occasion when the Duke of Monmouth was literally run to earth after the disastrous battle of Sedgemoor. His subsequent execution was

breeders managed, however, to keep a dozen hounds alive and, from this small nucleus, breeding began again after the war was over. Then in 1949 fresh blood was imported from Canada and the noble hound was once again on the increase, this time largely as a show dog and for use in competitive field trials.

Elin Richards, an expert breeder of Bloodhounds, explained to us how these trials work. The human 'victim' walks a trail and then, some hours later, that person's scent is given to the dog, from a cloth that has been carried on the 'victim's' body. The Bloodhound is then timed in its tracking of the trail to the finishing point. A novice dog will be asked to track a scent that is half an hour old, over a distance of one mile. Expert dogs are required to track a scent that is twenty-four hours old, over a distance of three miles. Amazingly, the three-mile distance has been covered successfully in as little as eighteen minutes.

These feats of detection are all the more impressive when it is realized that the trail can be criss-crossed by other people walking this way and that, without putting off the dogs. They totally ignore the other scents, no matter how strong they may be. This quality is called being 'free from change'.

Perhaps the most extraordinary feature of these tracking abilities is that the Bloodhounds can follow a human scent even when the person concerned is wearing wellington boots. Despite the fact that all foot odour is completely eliminated by the rubber boots, the dogs can still track down their quarry. We asked Elin Richards how on earth this can be done and she explained that, as a human being walks along, tiny particles of human scent fall from all over the body, down on to the ground 'like invisible dandruff'. The microscopic 'scales of scent' are quite enough for the huge nose of the Bloodhound to follow. It is little wonder that they have proved so successful in tracking down their human prey.

If you are a criminal on the run, however, there is one good piece of news in this otherwise bleak prospect. Once the Bloodhounds have caught up with you as you lie gasping and exhausted in a ditch, they are most unlikely to sink their large teeth into your aching limbs. Instead the chances are that they will cheerfully lick your face, being so pleased to see you after such a long and arduous chase.

therefore directly due to the Bloodhound's almost infallible sense of smell.

As the deer-parks began to disappear, the huntsmen were forced to turn their attentions to foxes. This change required a swifter hunting dog and one was created by crossing the Bloodhound (for its nose) with the Greyhound (for its speed). The result was called a Foxhound and in popularity it soon almost eclipsed the ancient, noble Bloodhound. Fortunately there was a new task for the old breed, that of tracking down poachers. So all was not lost.

In the New World, Bloodhounds had been imported to pursue first Indians, then runaway slaves and finally escaped criminals. These tasks prevented the breed from becoming extinct, although in recent years its popularity has waned considerably because of improved techniques in pursuing a man on the run. Also, of course, the fleeing man is far less likely to be on foot, and even Bloodhounds cannot track down getaway cars.

In Britain during the Second World War, the breed had all but vanished. Two enthusiastic

The Most Valuable Fish in the World

The highest price ever paid for a fish is an amazing £140,000. This huge sum was handed over for a champion specimen of the ornamental Japanese carp known as Koi. To the inexpert eye these beautiful Koi carp look like large goldfish but they do not, in fact, belong to the same species. A closer look at the head region reveals that Koi have two small barbels hanging down, one from each mouth-corner – goldfish lack this feature. Once you get to know it, you soon realize as well that the Koi carp has a very different personality from the humble goldfish. It is more restrained, more intelligent and more selective in the way it reacts to people, altogether a more complicated character. By contrast, the goldfish bumbles along, a greedy, happy-go-lucky, simple-minded fish.

To own a Koi is like owning a Rolls-Royce – you feel an immediate respect for its special qualities. Koi enthusiasts soon become hopelessly addicted to this strangely hypnotic fish. When we spoke to Doug Sargent, who has been keeping Koi at his home for thirty-five years

Doug Sargent shows Sarah his Koi carp

and now has around a hundred of them, he told us of the enormous pleasure he derives simply from sitting and watching them. Nearly every evening he spends between two and three hours with them in the specially-converted conservatory at the back of his house. There he has constructed two ponds, the larger one about 6 feet deep in which he keeps about thirty of his biggest Koi, most of them around 2 feet in length and valued at at least £1,000 each. The smaller fish in the other pond are worth about £450 each, making the whole collection a major investment.

Koi are slow-growing fish, taking about eight years to reach maturity and then living, it is claimed, for as long as two hundred years if they avoid any unusual mishaps. But they are not easy to breed and many of the very young fish die unless they are given special attention. The problem appears to be that in their first winter they often succumb to the cold, not having grown fast enough to build up the body weight needed to pass through the non-feeding phase of winter. So all Doug's valuable Koi have been imported from Japan, where they have centuries of experience in caring for this particular kind of fish.

The ancestor of the domesticated Koi is the Common carp, a fish that has been bred for food since at least 470 B.C. The earliest record of it comes from China, but it was also popular in the fishponds of great houses and monasteries throughout Europe from at least the fifth century A.D. It was fed largely on kitchen refuse and provided a valuable source of protein at times when game was scarce. Its domestication in the West and the East seems to have developed separately and with different conclusions. In the West, as soon as transportation systems improved and sea fish became available inland, the carp ponds went into a rapid decline as a major source of food. In the East, before this could happen, a new trend grew out of the old one. Brightly-coloured mutations began to appear and attracted attention for purely aesthetic reasons.

The Japanese, with their longstanding interest in decorative gardens, were fascinated by these multi-coloured fish and began to inter-

breed them to intensify their colours and improve their looks still further. The dull old mud-coloured Common carp, known locally as *Ma-goi*, was gradually overshadowed in importance by these flashy newcomers, christened 'Koi'. Traditional food ponds became exotic ornamental ponds.

The oldest record we have of the cultivation of Koi in Japan is in a text dating from nearly eighteen hundred years ago. We also know that a few centuries later the Koi were considered noble fish and were the favourites of the Japanese nobility. As the years passed they inevitably acquired a mystical, legendary reputation. It was said that they were the only fish that could swim up the Ryumon Falls of the Yellow River and this incredible capacity made them symbols of strength and, above all, of masculinity. Right up to the present time there has been an annual celebration on the fifth of May, the Boys Day Festival, when families fly a giant paper or cloth image of the Koi – sometimes as much as 20 feet long – to symbolize their hope that their sons will be as strong and tenacious as the magnificent Koi carp. So the possession of a Koi is not merely the ownership of an attractive fish, it is also the stewardship of a magical phallic symbol, steeped in centuries of oriental tradition and reverence. This may account, to some extent, for the vast sums paid for the very best of the champion Koi – the ones used in competitions that are followed in Japan

with a passionate fanaticism. In some circles, to own the biggest and best Koi is the greatest masculine status symbol of all. Not for nothing is the Koi referred to in hushed tones as 'The Warrior's Fish'.

For those who feel the urge to plunge into the extravagant world of Koi-keeping there must be a few words of warning. An ordinary goldfish pond is not enough for these aristocrats of the fish world. Ideally they require a depth of about 5 feet of water. This water should be aerated, filtered and provided with a current. In addition there should be shaded areas and water plants. Anyone who is prepared to go to these lengths will, however, be greatly rewarded. Their large size when fully grown – up to 30 inches – makes them an impressive sight. There are unicoloured Koi in red, white, black, silver and gold, and multicoloured ones in almost every conceivable combination of these colours, each with its own special Japanese name, such as Kohaku, Taisho-Sanke, Kin-Ki-Utsuri. The precise, map-like distribution of the colours is unique to each individual fish, so that there is a constant fascination in trying to find yet another Koi that will be just that bit more exquisite than the others – a search that drives the Japanese fanatics to outlandish extremes of competition at their Koi carp championship shows. Little wonder that they refer to the Koi as the 'living jewels' of Japan, for they not only look like bright jewels, they also cost as much.

The Dog on the Bed

Many dogs try to share their owners' beds. Few succeed. For most people there is a limit to the extent to which they are prepared to share their lives with their pet animals, no matter how deep the attachment. For most dogs, the rejection from the bed-covers is hard to understand, for they have descended from pack-living wolves, where sleeping close together is a natural part of their social lives.

There are, however, a few dogs that seem to have been developed specifically as boudoir companions, or pillow dogs. These favoured breeds have, from ancient times, been allowed to go wherever their privileged mistresses have gone, never being permitted to stray far from their sides. For this purpose they had to be extremely small, clean, healthy and beautiful. The dog that first filled this role – and for many owners fills it still – is the little Maltese. Popular as a lap-dog for several millennia, it never appears to have had any other function beyond delighting its high-born owners, in ancient Egypt, Greece and Rome, and in medieval Europe, right through to the present day, when its popularity is steadily mounting.

This dog is often referred to as the Maltese terrier, but it is safer not to use this name within the hearing of a Maltese enthusiast. For the suggestion that this diminutive aristocrat of the dog world could possibly have begun its life as a mere working terrier – a digger and ratter – is considered highly insulting. Other lap-dogs, like the little Yorkshire terrier, may be ex-ratters acting the role of companion dogs, but the noble Maltese has never had to soil its delicate paws on anything so mundane as scratching in the earth for a living. It is a palace pooch, through and through, and shows this lofty background in its bearing and personality. So say the Maltese owners, and looking at these

The Maltese – a high-status lap-dog

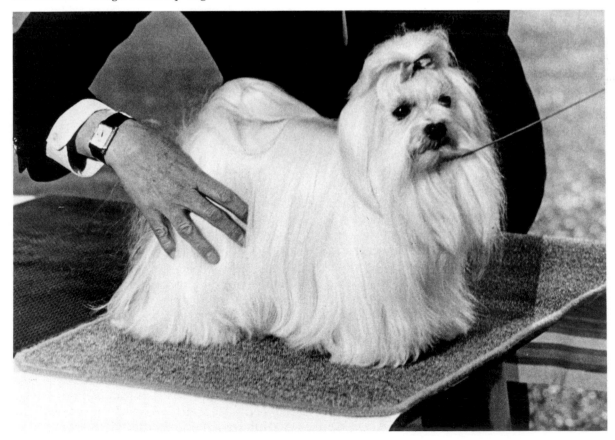

15

In Dr Caius's famous book *Of English Dogges*, published in 1576, there is a long passage describing, in scolding tones, the way in which these little dogs were pampered by their wealthy owners: '. . . the smaller they be the better they are accepted and the more pleasure they provoke as play-fellows for mincing mistresses to beare in their bosoms . . . to succour with sleepe in bed and nourish with meat . . . to lie in their laps and licke their lips . . .'

Those extremely small individuals are no longer popular, the average show size being between 6 and 9 pounds. And their owners are no longer 'mincing mistresses', but serious enthusiasts who consider the breed to be both intelligent as a companion and alert as a watch-dog, in addition to being strong and hardy without making heavy demands for exercise. In fact, the ideal urban dog for the present day.

attractive dogs it is hard to disagree with them.

Although descriptions, pictures and statues of these dogs make it clear that they have been around for many centuries, it is not so clear why they should have acquired the name Maltese. People living on the island of Malta have rarely if ever seen one of them. Yet to the ancient Greeks they were known as the 'Melitean lap-dogs', from which it has been concluded that they came then from the island called Melita, which is modern-day Malta. It has been thought that they started on that island and then, long ago, died out there. But this does not fit with the facts, for they were known in Ancient Egypt at a much earlier date, when it is most unlikely that the Maltese would have been concerned with a tiny lap-dog for noblewomen.

A more likely explanation is that the Greek name meant 'sweet dog'. The Greek word for honey is *meli*, and it was used by the ancients in naming the island of Malta because it was renowned for producing sweet honey. It is possible that all the Greeks were saying about their small white dogs is that they were as sweet as honey, rather than that they came from the 'honey island'. It would, however, be easy for such an error to be made as the small palace dog spread across early Europe, and mistakes, once made, can survive tenaciously for hundreds of years.

Sarah meets Maltese expert Muriel Lewin

Muriel Lewin, who has been breeding and judging Maltese at shows for the last thirty years, told us that, for her, the appeal of the Maltese could be summed up in a single word: glamour. And watching these dogs as they move elegantly around the show-ring it is easy to see what she means.

The Llama Farmer

Enter George Walker's farm near Horsham and you can be forgiven for imagining that you have suddenly switched continents. Instead of sheep and cattle in his fields, there are llamas, guanacos and alpacas – all South American mammals more at home in the Andes than in the West Sussex countryside.

We asked George how he made the decision to break so drastically with English agricultural traditions and become a llama farmer. He explained that it all began by accident. Originally he and his father ran an ordinary dairy farm but then added an export quarantine station. About three years ago a male llama was delivered there in error and the Walkers decided that it would be cheaper to keep it on their farm than to return it to the zoo where it had originated. They became attached to the animal and started checking into the possibility of using it as a kind of giant sheep and shearing its thick wool on a commercial basis.

They discovered that Britain imports mil-

lions of pounds' worth of llama wool from South America each year, and they decided to go into business. They now have more than thirty llamas, acquired one by one from zoos with a breeding surplus. And they have also acquired a few guanacos, the wild ancestor of the domestic llama, and some alpacas, for experimental cross-breeding.

Llama wool is renowned for its strength and softness and the Walkers have just carried out their first annual shearing. It proved to be something of a challenge. Catching the animals was easier than they thought it would be, but the actual shearing process was much more difficult. Unlike sheep, who react sheepishly to the ordeal of the clippers, the llamas decided they would have none of it and became, as George put it, 'rather boisterous'. The solution was to administer a mild sedative and then all was well. After that it was like clipping a horse, rather than true sheep-shearing, because the wool tended to come away in clumps instead of

Llama (right) meets alpacas on an English farm

as a complete fleece. This is because, compared with a sheep's wool, it lacks oil and has no lanolin. Llamas are sheared with pneumatic shears as the conventional type become too hot. George believes that there is a great future for this type of farming and that in the years ahead we will see more and more llama farms springing up in this country.

At present there are 3.7 million llamas in the world, 70 per cent of them in Bolivia. Back at the time of the Spanish conquest of the New World there were also huge numbers. There were no fewer than 300,000 of them working in the silver mines alone, and countless thousands more throughout the ancient civilizations of South America. In fact, the fabulously affluent society of the Incas was based on the 'slave labour' of the herds of llamas, which operated as beasts of burden and message-carriers across a complex and highly advanced network of roadways. The method employed to send messages was called the *quipus* and consisted of tying a complicated series of knots in the long fur hanging down from the undersides of the animals.

George Walker, following in the footsteps of the Incas

Desmond and Sarah meet a llama at the Zoologica show

Surprisingly the llama has one of the longest histories of domestication of any species. Archaeologists in Peru have recently been able to trace its exploitation by man back to 5500 B.C.

For the ancient Peruvians it was a multi-purpose creature. As a pack animal it could carry loads of up to 100 pounds for 15 miles a day. In addition, its dung was used as fuel, its tallow for candles, its flesh for meat, its rather poor milk for drinking, its hide for sandals, and its fur for rugs and rope. Clothing, however, was made from the wool of its smaller relative, the alpaca, because of that animal's finer hairs, and this is the reason that the Walkers have recently added a few alpacas to their collection. By crossing the two types of animal they have high hopes that they will be able to create a new, improved wool that will open up an even bigger market. If they succeed we may well start noticing more and more strange animal faces peering at us over the hedges and fences of the British countryside. It is an attractive prospect and the Walkers are to be congratulated on refusing to accept the rather rigid farming traditions that have so limited the kinds of livestock previously seen in Britain.

The Dog between the Wheels

Few dogs have had as many names as the flashy Dalmatian. It has been called the Spotted Dick, the Plum Pudding dog, the Coach dog, the Firehouse dog, the Stable dog, the Clown dog and, most recently, the Dally. Strangely, its official name of Dalmatian is the most difficult to understand because the breed does not come from Dalmatia – despite the fact that most dog books unthinkingly claim that it does. Dalmatia is part of modern-day Yugoslavia and the native population there knows nothing about the dog. In the 1950s some German enthusiasts made a thorough search of that part of the world, showing photographs of Dalmatians to all the local people they met. They drew a blank until they came to Dubrovnik, where they were excited to find someone who could show them 'the last Dalmatian in Dalmatia'. It was indeed a Dalmatian, an eight-year-old male, and it seemed as if, at last, the origin of the breed had been traced. Unfortunately, questioning produced a surprising answer. It turned out that the dog was the last surviving descendant of a group of Dalmatians that had been *imported* into Dalmatia by a millionaire shipowner in the 1930s. Apparently he had felt it his duty to take Dalmatians back to the place from which they were supposed to have started as a breed. So their origin remains obscure.

One theory about their beginnings sees them as gypsy dogs that accompanied Romany caravans, starting in Asia and then moving more and more to the West. Another pictures them as dogs of war, running into battle beside the horses of the warriors. Both these roles would have been appropriate precursors for the main duty that was to develop for this breed when it reached Western Europe: that of the ornamental coach dog.

As coach dogs, Dalmatians essentially provided a status display. With their glamorous, black-spotted, white bodies striding along beside a nobleman's coach, they created a splendid image of ostentatious wealth. Some were trained to run alongside the coach, others, with difficulty, to run just in front of it, and still others beneath the rear axle. It was the dogs between the wheels that were considered the very pinnacle of fashion in the days when elaborate coach travel was the best way of displaying one's social importance to all and sundry.

The stamina of these dogs was amazing. In the middle of the last century it is recorded that a Dalmatian ran a distance of 72 miles, on a winding course between Brighton and London, on eight successive days. Like so many Dalmatians he preferred to run very close to the heavy wheels and tragically this was eventually his undoing. One day he fell under one of them and was killed. He was so famous by this time that he was stuffed and put on show in a pub in the Edgware Road, to remind people of his devotion to duty and his extraordinary staying power.

It is this staying power that modern owners of Dalmatians have been known to curse under

Another possible reason for its unjustified reputation for stupidity is that, back in its working days, it was always housed with the horses, so that it would become completely at ease with them and could kill the rats and mice that infested the stables. This meant that it was out of touch with its owners, who only encountered the Dalmatian when out on coach-trips. So it is not surprising that the breed failed to develop an intelligent relationship with the people who kept it. Even when a coach arrived at its destination, away from home, the coach dogs were not rewarded indoors, for it then became their task to stand guard over the valuable carriage of their master.

Today, Dalmatian owners speak glowingly of the breed's exuberance, inquisitiveness and character, and are fiercely defensive of its good qualities. As one owner put it, these dogs are not only beautiful to look at but also beautiful to be with. A walk with a Dalmatian is a cure for depression . . .

Mrs Greening has bred Dalmatians for twenty-five years

their breath occasionally when their pets, after immensely long and exhausting walks, look up at them with an expression that says, 'When are we going to get started?'

With the arrival of the modern motor car, the breed nearly became extinct. But its delightful appearance and its obedient, friendly disposition have kept it going as a show dog and a pet breed. In 1961, when Walt Disney released his film *One Hundred and One Dalmatians*, its popularity soared again.

A weakness of the breed, many people believe, is that it is a particularly stupid animal. This is far from the truth, but the opinion was probably first formed because many Dalmatians used to suffer from deafness. Misunderstood, they could easily have been falsely accused of stupidity. Deafness is still a problem with these dogs, but it is gradually being brought under control by selective breeding.

Learning to Go Ape

Nine-year-old Martina Hardacre had never met a chimpanzee or a gorilla in the flesh before. She told us she had been looking forward to it all week, but it is doubtful if she was prepared for what happened when Molly Badham, the director of Twycross Zoo, brought in two of her young apes, a twenty-month-old chimpanzee called Becky and a young gorilla of the same age called Asante (which is Swahili for 'thank you').

At first, the two young apes eyed us suspiciously and approached with caution. They were taking no chances with perfect strangers. We offered Becky the correct chimpanzee greeting by pressing the back of a limp hand against the young ape's lips. Our greeting was accepted and in a few minutes Becky was running around and playing in a more relaxed way with Asante.

The moment had come to try and teach Martina how to communicate in chimp. There is no point in talking to apes in English. The best they can glean from our speech is our general tone of voice – is it harsh, or soft, or whining? This can give them a clue about our general mood, but little more. If we want to go beyond this we have to use the noises that the chimpanzees make when they encounter one another in natural social groups.

There is a special feeding noise, AAGH AAGH AAGH; a deep greeting noise, UGH UGH UGH; a cry of mild alarm, OOUGH OOUGH OOUGH; a whimper of distress, OOOOU OOOOU OOOOU; and a loud, long-distance greeting, OUG-AH OUG-AH OUG-AH. We took some food that Molly Badham had given us and, pretending to eat it, started making the food noise. The little chimp gave us a sharp look for a moment but then returned to the more serious business of playing with the gorilla. Next we made the greeting sound. Martina was sitting next to the young chimp and when she leaned close to its head, making the soft UGH UGH UGH noise, she was amazed to find the animal react immediately by turning

Martina Hardacre begins her first lesson in speaking chimpanzee

round towards her and flinging a pair of long, hairy arms around her neck. It was a moment of mutual acceptance and quickly led to a boisterous bout of physical play that left Martina gasping.

The real problems began for her when the young gorilla, feeling left out and perhaps even a little jealous of this new relationship between Becky and Martina, came charging over and leapt up on to her shoulders. Jumping up and down there, he quickly asserted himself and became the dominant figure in the play relationship. Becky was a little put out by this and started slapping down on to Martina's body with the palms of her hands. The little girl had all but disappeared now beneath the two young apes, each competing for the attention of this new-found friend of theirs.

Throughout it all Martina kept smiling and never once showed any concern. The language of play-fighting is something that we share with the apes. It is easy for us to understand whether they are fighting in jest or for real. And easy for

them to understand if a young girl like Martina is a friendly playmate to be trusted, or not. So a bond of understanding was growing, minute by minute, between the girl and the apes and all three of them were relishing it, even though to outside eyes it looked rather rough and even brutal. After it was over, Martina said she had enjoyed every minute of it and had never been frightened, even when they were both jumping up and down on her at the same time. What she had discovered in her encounter with the two species closest to mankind was that the chasm that separates us from them may be deep but it is also very narrow. It is not so hard to reach across. All we have to do is to forget words, use grunts and above all employ our eyes. The visual body language of apes is in many ways similar to our own and it takes comparatively little effort to adapt to the slight differences.

Given more time, Martina would soon have learned how to 'go ape' and to strengthen the bond of understanding between her and her hairy friends. Then she would find it increasingly difficult to think of chimpanzees or gorillas as 'inferior species'. Instead she would come to see them as merely different from us, lacking in verbal communication, but with their own unique personalities and their own special kind of dignity.

The Dog of Unmatchable Courage

The very name 'Mastiff' has a sinister ring about it. Three hundred years ago Edward Topsel described this type of dog as '. . . vast, huge, stubborn, ugly, and eager . . . terrible, and frightful to behold . . . a kind of dog capable of courage, violent and valiant, striking cold fear into the hearts of men, but standing in fear of no man, in so much that no weapons will make him shrink, nor abridge his boldness . . . The force which is in them surmounteth all belief, the fast hold which they take with their teeth exceedeth all credit.'

It is little wonder that, with this impressive reputation, the Mastiff was the most prized guard dog in the British Isles in ancient times. Some authors have claimed that it originated in these islands, but that is not true. It began life, most probably, in the mountains of Asia and was brought from there to the first great civilizations of the Middle East, where it acted as a guard dog or a dog of war. Mediterranean traders are then thought to have brought it to Britain in the sixth century B.C. When Alexander the Great was making his journeys eastward in the fourth century B.C. he also acquired these great dogs. Some were taken back to Macedonia where they were given the name 'Molossian dogs'. Later they were taken to Rome where they were employed in the arena at gladiatorial exhibitions.

The scene was now set for a strange confrontation. When the Romans landed in Britain they saw the British Mastiffs for the first time and were astonished. It used to be thought that they were amazed because they had never seen such dogs before, but in reality their amazement was due to the quality of the British dogs, which far outshone anything back in Rome. This is not surprising. The Roman Mastiffs, arriving via Greece, had retained the slightly smaller size typical of dogs from hot countries. The British Mastiffs, by contrast, had already experienced several centuries of the much colder, northern climate of early Britain. As a result, they had developed into a much bigger, more massive breed and the Romans were quick to exploit this difference, initiating the very first canine export trade from this country.

The British Mastiffs, on being sent back to Rome, were pitted against the home-bred variety. The outcome was too uneven to be of much interest, especially as the home team always lost. The gigantic British dogs slaughtered the Roman Mastiffs with ease. Something tougher had to be found to confront them. It is recorded that in contests they were matched one to a gladiator, three to a bear and four to a lion.

In Britain, as the years passed, they were employed in a number of roles. Anglo-Saxon peasants used them to control the wolves that still roamed the British forests. For centuries they were given the unsavoury task of tormenting and torturing tethered bulls in the cruel sport of bull-baiting. In addition to these pit combats they were out in the hunting field helping in the pursuit of large game and were also to be found chained up outside many a property, as savage guard dogs.

Because of their ferocity, they were less successful in other walks of life. There is an popular, and now, today, the population is more stable, though still not numerous.

One breeder who is doing his best to keep the Mastiff going is Raymond Boatwright. He insists that despite its violent past the huge beast is today a gentle giant, a docile plodder which makes an excellent companion and is completely trustworthy with those it knows. Strangers are another matter, however, Mastiffs remaining the excellent guard dogs they have always been. As Raymond explained: 'If you drove up to my house, you wouldn't get out of your car.' Bearing in mind that he owns not one but twelve of these huge dogs, this is not so surprising. His favourite quote concerning the breed is from Sydenham Edwards's volume on British dogs published in 1800: 'What the lion is to the cat, the mastiff is to the dog . . .'

But perhaps the last word should go to William Shakespeare, who in *Henry V* makes a Frenchman say: 'That island of England breeds very valiant creatures: their mastiffs are of unmatchable courage.'

Raymond Boatwright keeps twelve Mastiffs

amusing reference to them in a 'Lament of a Poor Blind Man' by Thomas Hood: 'A Mastiff once led me about, but people appeared so to fear him, I might have got pence without his defence, but Charity would not come near him.'

When bull-baiting and bear-baiting were prohibited in the nineteenth century the popularity of the Mastiff went into decline. This decline continued until the breed reached near extinction. After the Second World War a survey revealed that there were only eight Mastiffs left in the whole of the British Isles. The solution was to import new blood from the United States, where the breed had remained more

A Lizard in the Lounge

To say that Henry Waldron has a lizard in his lounge is an understatement. In the front room of his small house in the centre of Stafford there is hardly room for anything *but* lizards. What little space there is to spare is taken up by bird-eating spiders, turtles, scorpions, toads and large tropical fish. There is no corner left for his ferrets, which must stay out in the garden, or his dogs, which must make do with the rest of the house.

You will gather from this that Henry is an animal fanatic. Like so many people who enjoy the company of other species – and who would feel quite naked if not surrounded by them – he has been passionate about animals since early childhood. It is a form of early conditioning that seems almost impossible to break. Once an animal-man, always an animal-man. And for Henry it has been reptiles that have been at the centre of his obsession.

For some reason, amateur herpetologists usually focus their attention on snakes and it is quite uncommon to find someone who has specialized instead in lizards. Snakes do, of course, have a dramatic impact on visitors and this is often part of their appeal. The snake-handler is looked upon with amazement by those who fear snakes. But for Henry it is the sheer beauty of the lizards that attracts him and he is sensibly more interested in studying his animals than shocking his friends.

Pride of his collection is a 4-foot-long Bengal monitor. With its long head and neck, heavy body, thick tail and powerful legs equipped with intimidating claws, it looks rather like a small dragon. And when it flicks out its very long, forked tongue it momentarily gives the impression of breathing fire. It is easy to imagine how sailors' tales in earlier days could have exaggerated the size of this reptile to help keep alive the legend that '. . . here be dragons!'

Although the monitors are true lizards, in three respects they are more like snakes than other, more typical, lizards. The forked tongue is the first and most obvious of these snake-like features. Secondly, they have lost the ability to shed their tails when attacked. This is a common trick of most lizards when grabbed or bitten by an enemy. The predator is left with a wriggling tail in its mouth, while the rest of its intended prey scampers off otherwise unharmed, to re-grow its missing tail at leisure. Snakes and monitors have lost this ability, snakes because their tails are so important to them for locomotion, and monitors because their tails have become so thick and massive that to shed one would involve a major amputation. Thirdly, monitors, like snakes, swallow their prey whole instead of first chewing it up, and they have each developed a powerful, bony roof to the mouth to prevent damage to the brain when hard objects (such as turtles) are being swallowed.

In captivity monitors become remarkably tame and display little objection to being handled. It is claimed that they soon get to know their owners and will even learn to answer to their names. And there is no danger of losing them, because they have a well-developed homing ability. If they do take off on an unscheduled expedition they can easily find their way back, over distances of at least 500 yards.

In addition to his huge monitor, Henry also owns a Mexican Spiny-tailed iguana, a Common iguana, and a large Blue-tongued skink. The iguanas, with their spiky crests, look like

Blue-tongued skink

Iguana

small replicas of the monsters from the dinosaur age. The skink is a smooth-skinned, fat-bodied, thick-tailed lizard with a remarkable defence mechanism. When threatened, it opens its jaws wide and gapes frighteningly at its enemy with its highly-coloured mouth, its cobalt-blue tongue contrasting markedly with its red mouth-lining.

While Henry was showing us his favourite lizards he was concentrating so hard on holding them correctly for our cameras that he hardly noticed the damage that their sharp claws were doing to his hands. Afterwards we realized that the backs of his hands and his wrists were livid with red scratch-lines and dripping with blood. But he shrugged it off as of no consequence. Far more important to him had been the opportunity to convey to others the fascination of reptiles, a fascination that will doubtless absorb him for as long as he lives.

A Dog in the Lap

For thousands of years domestic dogs have worked hard for their living, hunting, herding, fighting, guarding, searching and guiding, not to mention pulling sledges, performing tricks, sniffing out drugs and acting in films. These are all active pursuits requiring a great deal of muscular energy and the various breeds involved have responded magnificently to the demands put upon them. Sometimes their tireless devotion to duty has been almost beyond belief.

The owners of such dogs are exploiting their ancient 'pack loyalty', derived from their distant ancestry as wolves. Members of a wolf pack can only survive if they act as a co-operative group, hunting down their large prey in a combined operation. So the urge to help one another and to co-operate with the pack leader is deeply ingrained in both the wolf and its domestic descendant, the dog. Playing on this quality of group loyalty, a ruthless human owner can make impossible demands on his working dogs and they will do their utmost to comply.

There has been a working role for dogs since the neolithic age, but as the centuries have passed there has grown up another, totally different, role: that of simple companion. Not all dog owners have been ruthless, even in the earliest days of domestication. Many have responded with loving affection for their canine partners. For man, too, has evolved as a co-operative hunter and has an inborn urge to aid the other members of his social group. This has often included his dogs, and the strong bonds of attachment have worked both ways.

In the first instance this attachment led to playful puppies being treated as companions by young children, before both were thrust out into the demanding world of adult work and survival. But these puppies also had strong appeal for human females, arousing their powerful maternal instincts and protective urges. If mutations occurred, giving rise to unusually small dogs which remained 'puppy-sized' even when adult, such animals managed to keep their appeal, even when fully-grown. A few of these, even back in the Stone Age, may well have been kept simply as family pets. Such instances may have been rare in those early days, but as civilization progressed and there was an increasing division of labour, the demand for them must have increased. As soon as there were courts and palaces, with female inhabitants enjoying freedom from drudgery, the little companion dog came into its own.

It seems that it was the ancient Egyptians who were first to breed a miniature dog suitably scaled down to the weight of a human baby and therefore ideal for cuddling and holding in the arms as an adored child-substitute. Small figures of toy dogs of the kind we today call Maltese were found in the tomb of Rameses II, Egyptian ruler from 1290 to 1223 B.C. It is likely that the Egyptians originally obtained long-haired dogs from colder, northern countries and then miniaturized them as lap-dogs for females of high standing. From there, these prized little creatures spread out to the Greek and Roman worlds. The Greek Sybarites pampered them shamelessly and allowed them to share their opulent beds. A comic play of the period mentions a promise to give a dog 'a soft bed with a purple counterpane, to feed him well on gruel mixed with the yolks of ducks' eggs and to anoint his feet with a sweet-smelling oil'.

The Pekinese

The Romans were equally besotted, often writing sentimental poems to their favourite pet dogs: '. . . If she whimpers you'll think that she is speaking, sorrow and joy she feels as much as he does, snuggling close to his neck she sleeps so softly, that you'd scarcely believe the pet was breathing . . . Modest and chaste a little lap-dog is she . . .'

As the centuries passed, the tiny, cosseted lap-dog was to become a prestige gift, from nobility to nobility and court to court. In the days of Elizabeth I, by which time they had become known as 'spaniel-gentles', they were frowned upon as symbols of effete extravagance: '. . . to satisfie the delicateness of daintie dames and wanton women's witts, instruments of folly for them to play and dally withal . . .' These dogs were called 'comforters' and the smallest ones were worn as part of female costume.

Bichon Frise

It took a king – Charles II – to make it fashionable for males to join the females in their open adoration of the little lap-dogs. His palace was overrun with small dogs and they were given such priority by the monarch that his court became scandalized by his excesses. Pepys recorded that the king's pets '. . . made the whole court nasty and stinking.' Despite the court's feelings, the lap-dog was firmly established. And despite the outrage of his bishops,

Charles insisted that his beloved 'spaniel-gentles' should be present on his death-bed, to see him fondly into the next world.

Right up to the present time the dwarf companion dog has held its own and today demands a whole class to itself – the toy breeds – at major dog shows. They are no longer exclusive dogs of the royal courts and have lost their high status appeal, but their popularity has not diminished. Indeed, it has grown. This is because, in an increasingly urban world, where dog owners so often lack open spaces to exercise the larger breeds, the dwarf dogs can thrive. As cities continue to grow, small dogs will undoubtedly become more and more favoured.

In the past, toy dogs and lap-dogs have had several secondary uses. At one stage they were employed as 'flea decoys' to attract human fleas from wigs and complex costumes towards their hot skins. And they were thought to act as cures for various diseases, their bodies, if worn or held close, drawing out the poison from their human hosts. In the freezing buildings of earlier centuries they also played the role of living hot-water bottles, to keep their owners warm. All these functions have gone now, but the dogs remain, still held in loving arms. Their more basic appeal, as infant substitutes, survives. They give affection and arouse parental love and, in so doing, provide rewards for millions of owners the world over. Puritanical critics continue to scoff at these human/dog relationships, as they have done for years. They see them as 'trifling away the treasure of time', to quote a criticism from the earlier Elizabethan period. Human emotions, they believe, should be reserved exclusively for other humans and not 'wasted' on dumb animals. This assumes, of course, that human loyalty, love and devotion is always superior to that of our canine companions. Many people might doubt this and if they succeed in developing a deep emotional relationship with a pet dog they should be congratulated rather than condemned. For lap-dogs are not merely child-substitutes – they are also lively, intelligent companions that often bring out the best in their human owners.

Mark Twain once remarked: 'If you pick up a starving dog and make him prosperous, he will not bite you. This is the principal difference between a dog and a man.' If dogs can teach us the value of trust, when our own world is full of betrayal, that alone is worth their keep.

The Cat with a Curly Coat

There is far less variety among pedigree cats than among pedigree dogs. Because of this, cat breeders are always on the look-out for exciting mutations that may lead to the establishment of distinctive lines new to the 'Cat Fancy'. One such mutation occurred in Cornwall in 1950 and immediately created a stir in the cat world. The Rex cat had arrived.

The animal in question went by the delightful name of Kallibunker. He had a short, curly coat that marked him out from all other cats and which gave his new breed its name. This was not because he looked like a king, but because his fur was reminiscent of that of wavy-coated Rex rabbits. He also had a curious, wedge-shaped head and long slender legs, with those at the back even longer than the front ones. His ears were huge and pointed, with wide openings, looking rather like those seen on feline statues from ancient Egypt.

Kallibunker's strange form led to suggestions that perhaps his ancestors had been brought to Cornwall in ancient times by

The extraordinary Rex cat

Phoenician traders visiting the famous local tin mines. There is no proof of this, but his slender figure is certainly in stark contrast to that of the typical, sturdily-built British cats. He has a rangy look as though from a hot country such as North Africa, and his coat is also extremely sparse for a European cat.

Kallibunker was mated with his mother to produce the new Cornish Rex line. Two of the kittens were sent to the United States to establish the line there and, although it has never become a widely popular form of pedigree cat, it has always found enthusiasts prepared to keep its unusual qualities alive.

Once one pedigree curly-haired cat had become established, other isolated examples began to turn up elsewhere. In East Germany, the German Rex emerged, and when this was later crossed with the Cornish Rex it was found that they carried the same 'curly gene' and produced curly-coated offspring. Nearer home,

29

in Devon, another curly kitten was born and christened 'Kirlee'. It was naturally assumed to be genetically related to its Cornish neighbour, but when Kirlee was crossed with a Cornish Rex the resulting kittens were all straight-haired. Amazingly, the distant German Rex was the result of the same mutation as the Cornish, but the Devon Rex was a completely different, distinct breed, despite its superficial similarity and close proximity.

In the United States more curly-haired cats were discovered: the Marcel cat, with longer, wavy hair, was the most striking of these. In Holland there was a mutation with a rather coarse, wavy coat having a more bristly texture than the others. Now that curly coats have become a focus of interest, we will no doubt be seeing more and more of these mutants appearing around the globe, some of which will be carefully preserved and others allowed to fade away. How many should be kept is a matter of debate. In the cat world the Rex breeds cause heated arguments and divide experts into two strongly-opposed camps. The pro-Rex faction point out that they have fascinating personalities. They are said to retain their juvenile inquisitiveness and playfulness into adulthood to an unusual degree. And it is claimed that, remarkably, they wag their tails like dogs when they are pleased. This feature, combined with the tight curliness of their coats, has earned them the nickname of 'Poodle cats'.

The anti-Rex faction find these skinny, angular cats ugly to look at and point out that kittens are often born with extremely sparse fur that makes them look diseased. In the end it is all a matter of taste. We asked George Gow, who has been breeding and judging Devon Rex cats for many years, why they appealed to him so much and he stressed the unusual friendliness of the breed. He finds them more affectionate, requiring more human love and

companionship than other feline breeds. They are also more active and, above all, have enormous appetites compared with other cats. Perhaps, in the end, it is due to the very strangeness of the curly-coated Rex cats that their many fans have fallen under their spell.

One point in their favour is that people who love cats but who cannot own one of the usual breeds, because of an allergic response to ordinary cat fur, should be able to keep a Rex cat. Apparently, the peculiar fur of these odd cats has not produced allergic symptoms in certain sufferers. Whether this applies to all individuals with this particular allergy is not, of course, known. But it is worth a try.

The Dog without a Bark

The Basenji is perhaps the strangest of all dog breeds. According to Mirrie Cardew, one of the world's top Basenji experts, it has four unusual features which set it aside from all other domestic dogs. First it yodels instead of barking. Second it washes itself like a cat. Third it lacks the typical doggy smell. And fourth it has only one breeding season a year instead of the normal two. Together these qualities make it an ideal pet and it is surprising that it is not more popular. According to Kennel Club records it is only 112th in popularity, which amazingly puts it into the rare breed category.

It is probably the absence of a loud bark that puts people off most, since it means that the dog cannot help to guard the home by raising the alarm when strangers arrive. But against this there is the enormous advantage for urban dog owners of having a pet that cannot disturb the neighbours. So perhaps with a little publicity we will see the Basenji rise to its rightful place in the canine popularity stakes. Certainly Mirrie Cardew believes that it makes the perfect companion, being intelligent, lively and adaptable.

Two explanations have been given as to why the Basenji lost its bark, assuming it ever had one. The first is a fanciful, tribal legend from its African homeland. The inhabitants of central Africa explain that the ancestor of the Basenji was an animal called Rukuba who was so clever that it could speak. Being such an articulate speaker, Rukuba was given the task of being an official messenger. This entailed making many boring and exhausting trips, so the animal decided to give up talking altogether. By remaining silent it was spared its arduous duties and its descendants have remained silent ever since. Hence the barkless Basenji.

A more factual explanation is that the central

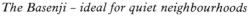

The Basenji – ideal for quiet neighbourhoods

ing terrier, or the Zande dog. Then, when serious attempts were made in the 1920s and 1930s to import breeding stock to Britain, it was given its final, official name of Basenji, meaning 'little thing of the bush'. It created a sensation when it first appeared at Crufts in 1937 and everyone predicted that it would soon become a top favourite dog breed. In 1939 the Basenji Club of Great Britain was formed 'to show the Western world what a fascinating dog the Basenji is'. Despite their efforts on behalf of this delightful breed, widespread popularity has yet to be achieved, but with increasing urbanization it will surely come.

African hunters wanted a dog that would remain silent during the tracking of prey, so that it could lead them near to the victims, using its excellent ability to pick up a scent at a distance of 250 feet, but without creating panic by excited barking. This explanation does not however apply everywhere, for in some regions the dog is employed in flushing game. For this it has to make a loud noise and, lacking a bark, has to be fitted with jangling bells around its neck.

In origin the Basenji has been traced back to ancient Egypt, where early carvings show a very similar animal in the period between 2700 and 2600 B.C. Perhaps it was the ancient Egyptians themselves who bred the barkless dog, possibly for some religious or ritual reason. Unfortunately we have no records to help us decide, and the breed disappeared into obscurity until the 1860s, when explorers of the Dark Continent first started to remark on this unusual dog, so popular with the native tribesmen that a good specimen was prized more than a wife.

In Africa it went by many names. The explorers called it the Belgian Congo dog, or the Congo Bush dog, sometimes the Congo Hunt-

A final point of interest: the wild ancestor of all domestic dogs, the wolf, howls a great deal but rarely barks and it has only a single breeding season instead of the typical domestic dog's two seasons each year. Could the Basenji have retained these primitive features from its earliest domestication, or are they merely accidental similarities? At present we have no way of answering these questions, and a closer look at the details of Basenji behaviour by serious observers of animal ethology would certainly be of great interest.

The People who are Dog's Best Friends

Moira Anderson is best known for her beautiful voice, but the much-loved Scottish singer has recently become active in a new field. She is one of the distinguished patrons, along with Katie Boyle, Dulcie Gray and Michael Denison, of an important canine organization called PRO Dogs. PRO Dogs is a charity whose work is concerned with improving the image of the dog in modern society. One of its aims is to oppose the extremist group that hates dogs and depicts them as a disgusting pest in our towns and cities. This anti-dog lobby has grown in recent years, especially in the major urban centres, and its warped attitudes require some kind of answer. The best rebuff, however, is not to be negative but to make a positive attempt to improve dog-keeping to a point where it is above criticism. It is this positive approach that PRO Dogs has adopted.

Among its activities are educational schemes to eliminate careless dog-handling that leads to stray dogs, needless cruelty, and the fouling of public places. At the present time many thousands of unloved, unwanted dogs have to be destroyed each year, and PRO Dogs will not rest until these figures have been massively reduced.

PRO Dogs also does its best to promote schemes in which dogs are employed in a therapeutic role. This branch of the organization is called PAT – standing for PRO Dogs Active Therapy. They arrange for dogs to be taken into hostels, hospitals and old people's homes. With the sick and the lonely they find that the animals work wonders. The excitement of meeting the dogs and then patting and stroking them not only decreases the boredom of the patients but also actually improves their health. It does this by reducing stress and thereby lowering blood pressure. It is particularly beneficial in the case of patients with heart trouble and in some instances can even save lives.

If this sounds a little fanciful, it should go on record that, when special experiments were done with patients wired up to measurement devices, it was conclusively demonstrated that their blood pressure decreased dramatically and their stress levels dropped as soon as they started engaging in loving interactions with

Moira Anderson – a patron of PRO Dogs

friendly dogs. As they began to stroke them, hug them, chat gently to them and pat them, their internal physiology really did improve. These findings should make the anti-dog lobby think again, for it is an observation from which they cannot escape.

PRO Dogs also takes dogs into schools to educate the young in the proper care of man's best and oldest animal friend. And each year it gives Gold Medals as special awards for brave and outstanding individual dogs, such as Brumby, the sniffer dog who found over four million pounds' worth of illicit drugs in a single year.

The importance of the PRO Dogs organization will undoubtedly increase in the years ahead, as more and more misguided local politicians are bullied into tightening restrictions on companion animals. Modern housing is often said to be unsuitable for pet animals and people taking up residence on new estates may suddenly find themselves faced with the heartbreak of having their favourite pets destroyed.

33

To anyone who understands the importance of companion animals and the way in which they instil in us a reverence for animal life, it is clear that new housing that is unsuitable for pets is also unsuitable for humans. The attempt on the part of some architects and town planners to redesign our homes as hygienic prison cells will be seen, in retrospect, to have been one of the major crimes against humanity in the twentieth century. The attack on pets, and in particular dogs, is a small symptom of this malaise, but it is one that we should not ignore.

The emotions produced by the new prohibitions have been amazingly intense. One woman, a social worker and a mother of five children, went to Holloway Prison rather than give up her right to take her children and her dogs for walks in her local park. The park in question was in Burnley, the town where dogs were first banned from public grounds. A High Court judge offered to let her off if she would give an undertaking not to walk her dogs in the park, but she refused, despite the disruption this decision would bring to her life.

The day when our society turns a woman walking her dog into a criminal to be jailed is the day when PRO Dogs has a major task to confront. No wonder their slogan is not only DOGS ARE GOOD FOR PEOPLE but also DOGS DESERVE BETTER PEOPLE.

An Ape in the Hand

It is a sad fact that today an ape in the hand is worth two in the bush. The natural forest homes of orang-utans, gibbons, chimpanzees and gorillas are under ever-increasing threat. Despite brave attempts at conservation, these Great Apes surviving in their original habitats are at serious risk. In a few decades, if we are not very careful, they could become extinct in the wild. If this happens, the only hope for the future will be with the captive apes kept in zoos and wildlife parks around the world. In the past, unhappily, all too many of these zoos have kept their apes merely for show and have not made the extra effort needed to set up breeding colonies. The tragic figures of solitary gorillas or orangs, staring sullenly through heavy bars and wire-mesh, have depressed all the more sensitive visitors and made them feel that it is morally wrong to incarcerate such close and intelligent relatives of ours. A strong anti-zoo lobby has sprung up. Where does this leave the apes themselves? Decimated in the wild, prohibited in captivity, the future looks bleak.

Chimpanzees at the Twycross breeding colony

Not so, says Molly Badham, director of the East Midlands Zoological Society and the Twycross Zoo. There is a solution. The zoos must reform and become dedicated breeding establishments, whatever the cost. If they do not, public opinion will close them all down. They must stop being lazy and start taking responsibilities. Molly herself is a pioneer of the captive breeding of the Great Apes and her record speaks for itself. Since the 1970s she has successfully bred no fewer than ten orang-utans, ten chimpanzees, three gorillas, and somewhere between thirty and forty gibbons. Her chimpanzee colony, now one of the best in the world, at present numbers twenty-five animals. In addition she has a group of six gorillas, seven orangs and thirty-five gibbons. It is an impressive collection and she takes its future very seriously indeed.

She is the first to agree that, in an ideal world, there should be no captive apes. They should all be enjoying a trouble-free existence in their natural, tree-top homes. But since that cannot be, she feels entirely justified in keeping

35

Molly Badham with young apes bred at Twycross

her captive colony at Twycross, despite the anti-zoo feelings that are being expressed in the 1980s. She would unhesitatingly join with the zoo critics where *bad* zoos are concerned – zoos that simply put an animal into a bleak empty cage and leave it there with nothing to do. But she believes that it is possible, even with highly intelligent animals like apes, to provide a zoo environment that is sufficiently stimulating to keep the animals happily active and healthy . . . and reproducing. All that is needed is a little extra effort in understanding the needs of our closest relatives. Thanks to recent studies in the wild by such investigators as Jane Goodall and Dian Fossey, we know so much more now about what sort of social life these fascinating species enjoy in their forest retreats and we can re-create the right social groupings in captivity. If you visit Twycross, take a look up at the walls of the spacious inner enclosures. There you will see large television sets, supplied solely for the use of the apes. Apparently they love watching the pictures on the screen (especially Westerns) and, like us, find this form of entertainment a wonderful escape from boredom on long winter evenings.

While we were with Molly we met two of the latest additions to her growing colony. The youngest was a baby male chimpanzee called Flynn, aged only seven weeks. Flynn's mother having been less than perfect in her maternal care, the baby was being hand-reared by the zoo staff, but was to be quickly introduced to other young apes so that she would not become too 'humanized'. If not treated in this way she might have become so attached to humans that she would never again have wanted to know about the company of her own kind and this could have interfered with her own breeding success later in life. So it was vitally important that she should become an 'ape's ape' and not a 'person's ape' as she grew up. The other young animal we encountered was a small female orang-utan called Valentine, born in the zoo on St Valentine's Day, and eight months old at the time of our visit. As with Flynn she was being given as much opportunity as possible to play with others of her own kind, so that she too would develop into a well-adjusted adult ape.

Whatever the anti-zoo groups may say, there is no doubt that Molly Badham is one of the best friends the apes could wish for.

36

The Dog with Mahogany Hair

The gun-dog known to its originators as the *Modder Rhu* (Gaelic for Red setter) is one of the most elegant and colourful of all modern breeds. With its shining mahogany-red hair and its graceful, bounding movements, it is a constant pleasure to the eye and quickly enslaves all those who become involved with it. Judy Russell has been breeding Irish setters, as they are now internationally known, for over thirty years and is in no doubt that they are the loveliest dogs in existence. Her obsession is such that she freely admits that she relates better to her dogs than to people. Defiantly she comments: 'Some people think we dog enthusiasts are mad, but it is they who are mad.'

The all-red setter is a comparatively recent development, having first appeared as late as the end of the eighteenth century. And it was not until the middle of the nineteenth century that it became fully established and began to outnumber its predecessor, the Red-and-White setter. Since the red-and-white dogs were easier for hunters to follow with their eyes as the animals moved back and forth across the hunting field, it is hard to see what possible practical advantage there could have been in the development of the all-red version. The suggestion that the pure red coat helped to camouflage the dogs from their prey makes little sense when one reads that the early Irish hunters used to tie large white handkerchiefs around the animals' necks to make them more conspicuous. It would seem that the appeal of the red coat was, even then, purely aesthetic, and that from its very beginnings the Irish setter was bred for beauty.

Although the Irish setter is less than two hundred years old as a distinct breed, its closely-related ancestors can be traced back for centuries. Setters as a hunting type seem to have first been developed in the sixteenth century to help in the netting of birds. The word 'setter' means literally 'sitter', the original habit of the breed being to lie down and stay

The Red setter, one of the most handsome of all gundogs

Water spaniel, the Gordon setter, the English setter, the Springer spaniel, the Irish terrier and the Pointer. The problem is that, in the early days of hunting, comparatively little attention was paid to keeping true lines. The hunting dogs were repeatedly cross-breeding, and controlled breeding programmes were rare. But we can be fairly certain that the Pointer and spaniels of some kind were both involved in the original production of the modern setter.

Because the Irish setter has such energy and stamina on the hunting field, it is a highly unsuitable animal for confined city living. Its great popularity in the show-ring during the twentieth century has meant that many people have acquired these very active dogs and have then failed to give them the kind of exercise they demand. It is because of this that the breed has unfairly gained a reputation in certain quarters as being 'headstrong, excitable, boisterous, flighty and unreliable'. Given a country environment and miles and miles of exercise, it proves to be a companion that is 'sensitive, gentle, tireless, rollicking and good-humoured', to quote the addicted enthusiasts.

The ideal solution today for the breeders of champion dogs is to let them exercise like working dogs. This dual life keeps them in perfect condition, both physically and in terms of mood. If they are confined too much in their role as show dogs, their environment will cease to suit the temperament bred into them over the centuries, and they will suffer. Sadly for the urbanite, the handsome Irish setter will always have to remain a dog of the countryside if it is to retain its true, extrovert character.

still the moment it detects its prey. Like a Pointer, it remains stationary, aiming itself in the direction of the prey, until its hunting companions have taken action. A sixteenth-century report on the behaviour of this type of dog states: 'When he approcheth neere to the place where the bird is, he lays him downe and, with a marcke of his pawes, betrayeth the place of the byrdes last abode . . .' A later comment explains what happens next: 'The setter crouches down when it scents the birds, til the net be drawn over them.' This method of hunting having lost favour, the modern working setter is now used more as a general purpose gundog, stalking, pointing and retrieving the game for its master.

An earlier name for the Irish setter was the Red spaniel and it is clear that spaniels played an important role in its origins. Nobody is certain which breeds were involved in its manufacture, but strong contenders include the Irish

The Ugliest Dog in the World?

The amazing Shar-pei makes people stop and stare when they see it for the first time. Some are lost for words, while others feel compelled to attempt a description of its bizarre appearance. It has been called 'the dog wearing a coat three sizes too big', 'the dog with the face of a hundred-year-old peasant', and 'the dog that looks as though it has gone fifteen rounds with Muhammad Ali'. In the United States it regularly wins the 'Ugliest Dog Contest' and this is a source of great annoyance to Heather Sweeting, who is the secretary of the Chinese Shar-pei Club of Great Britain. She considers that, although this remarkable breed may not have the line and grace of a Borzoi or an Afghan hound, it does have a special kind of beauty all of its own. It is what someone once called 'ugly-beauty'.

The strangeness of its appearance is due to the heavy folds of its short-haired, bristly skin. In humans we expect wrinkles to increase with advancing age, but with the Shar-pei the opposite is the case. It is the puppies that show the greatest wrinkling. As they grow to adulthood, it is as if their bodies catch up with their coats in size, and the wrinkles become stretched out more and more. Even so, the skin remains remarkably loose when compared with that of other dogs.

The hair of the Shar-pei's short coat is harsh and not particularly pleasant to the touch. At its shortest it is only a quarter of an inch long and is then referred to as a 'horse-coat'. At its longest it is no more than an inch long and is then called a 'brush-coat', because it resembles a bristle hairbrush. The breed also has a most unusual padded muzzle, known as a 'meat-mouth', which gives it the head-shape of a hippopotamus.

In origin, the Shar-pei is closely related to the Chow Chow and these two Chinese breeds are the only ones in the whole of the domestic dog world that possess dark blue tongues. The Shar-pei was never a noble dog and was unlikely to have seen the insides of the ancient Chinese palaces, where the pampered Pekinese dogs lived in splendour. By contrast, it was the working dog of peasant farmers, used for hunting, protecting farm animals and guarding the

Shar-pei owners call their Club magazine 'The Wrinkle'

home. It was carrying out these duties as far back as the Han dynasty, about two thousand years ago, but later on its role changed dramatically: it became a fearsome fighting dog.

Gambling on brutal dog-fights was once a popular pastime in rural China and the Shar-pei was modified to suit this new role. In particular, it was selectively bred to have a skin so loose that its opponents could not stop it twisting and turning when they held it in their powerful jaws. The best Shar-pei was so loose-coated that it could spin round and bite its attacker while still firmly in its grip. It was this specialization as a fighter that led to the breed's present appearance, with the loose, folding coat becoming more and more exaggerated to improve the fighting stock. At the same time, its ears were bred smaller to avoid tearing, and its jaws and teeth heavier to improve biting. So the friendly, loving dog we see at dog shows today in reality obtained all its most appealing features for the worst of reasons.

Just ten years ago they were in danger of extinction

much for the Shar-pei in the fighting-ring, and their numbers decreased rapidly. Then in the present century China became strongly anti-dog. This eventually culminated with the Communist government banning the breeding of domestic dogs altogether. On mainland China the Shar-pei became virtually extinct. It survived only in a few small, isolated pockets – on offshore islands such as Macao and, importantly, in Hong Kong. It was there in Hong Kong that a rescue operation was mounted to save the breed from extinction. In the 1970s the *Guinness Book of Records* listed the Shar-pei as the rarest breed of dog in the world, but as a result of the efforts of a Hong Kong breeder called Matgo Law, its numbers began to increase. By the early 1980s, with help from American breeders, there were several hundred Shar-peis to be seen in the United States. Then in 1981 the first Shar-pei arrived in England and was followed by six more in 1982. During the past few years enthusiasts have bred from these animals until there are now well over a hundred Shar-peis in this country and the breed is certainly well and truly re-established. Its strange appeal is spreading further and further each year.

This history does not mean, however, that the Shar-pei is an untrustworthy breed that will fly at every dog it sees. On the contrary, its modern-day personality is calm and unruffled, slightly aloof with strangers, but very loyal and devoted to its owners. Without special training it would never savage another dog. It is important to realize that all fighting dogs have to be put through a specialized and brutal training period to make them truly savage and just because a particular breed has been developed for fighting purposes does not mean that a member of that breed will automatically be aggressive from birth. Treated as a much-loved family pet, any member of any breed – even the wolf itself – will become an affectionate, friendly companion. So there is nothing to fear from the modern Shar-pei, despite his gruesome history.

The breed nearly became extinct in recent years. To start with, its popularity began to wane in China in the nineteenth century when even more ferocious dogs were imported from the West. The Bulldog and the Mastiff were too

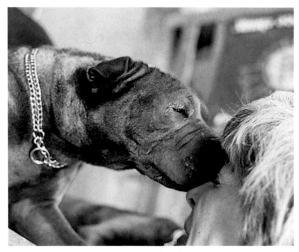

Today there are more than 100 in Britain alone

Owners of Shar-peis will tell you that the breed is remarkably intelligent. Historians have explained why this is so. It seems that in ancient China the less intelligent members of each litter were killed and eaten by their owners – an effective, if unattractive, way of rapidly increasing a breed's intellectual status.

On Being a Dog's Gentleman

Show dogs have become big business. The pedigree pups of top champions command increasingly high prices. So it comes as no surprise that professionals are beginning to move into what has for many years been an essentially amateur sphere. At major dog shows up and down the country it is now possible to see, among the many dog owners and breeders parading with their prize animals, a scattering of full-time, specialist dog handlers. Just as the human aristocrat has his 'gentleman's gentleman', so the nobility of the canine world now have their own 'dog's gentleman' to show them off to full advantage in the ring.

Geoff Corrish and his Irish partner Michael Coad are two of this new type of professional dog handler and they have become well-known faces at all the larger British dog shows. The old-style breeders view them with a mixture of admiration and disapproval. They like the importance that full-time professionals give to the show-ring, but they are also sometimes annoyed by the expert competition, and feel that the 'pros' may be at an advantage with the judges. This is because it is no secret that for a particular dog to be accepted by a professional handler it must be an exceptional individual. So the moment the 'pro' enters the ring the judge will automatically look upon his dog as an important one.

Persuading handlers like Geoff Corrish and Michael Coad to take on your dog is not easy. Many owners apply but only a few animals are accepted. A prospective dog is minutely examined and if it has even the slightest flaw it is politely refused. This is because, in addition to their own personal dogs, the two partners can only take on about ten show animals at any one time. So each dog must be physically near-perfect or it is not worth their while.

Once selected, the animal must leave the home of its owner and move in with the other 'professional dogs' at the kennels of its new managers. There, like a prize fighter, it will go into strict training. Diet is methodically controlled and improved to produce perfect coat condition; regular exercise ensures good muscle tonus; repeated grooming guarantees that the dog 'sparkles' on show days. The potential canine stars must remain at the pro-kennels for at least a year, sometimes longer, during which they are taken off in a group to each of the major shows.

Of particular importance during the training phase is the advanced education the dogs receive in good deportment. Like top fashion

Desmond meeting professional handler, Michael Coad

models they must learn to stand proudly, move gracefully and avoid all distractions, no matter how tempting they may be. At the very top level, where virtually all the dogs are physically without defect, it is often no more than a tiny difference in showiness that decides the winner. That extra bounce or prance, that firmness of stance or smoothness of gait, is the quality that resolves the conflict in the judge's mind. And it is on such subtleties that the pro-handlers concentrate most of their efforts.

Their success in the ring sometimes leads to

41

Dogs have to learn to 'sparkle' to catch a judge's eye

sharp envy and even hatred. Michael Coad told us that he once received a threatening telephone call just before a major competition. The anonymous caller told him to keep away from the show or his life would come to a sudden and painful end. He ignored it and needless to say all was well, but it is intriguing that feelings become so heated. We asked dog show officials whether this kind of threat was common. They explained that although the vast majority of dog owners and breeders who show their animals competitively do so in a friendly and straightforward way, it is inevitable, considering the huge numbers involved (sometimes as many as fifteen thousand dogs at one show) that there will be a few villains present. On rare occasions 'dirty tricks' do come to light, but they are nearly always directed at the dogs themselves rather than at the people with them.

It is unattended dogs that suffer and many people nowadays will not leave their show animals alone for a second. They either take them with them everywhere, or have a 'back-up friend' to help. Incidents that have occurred when dogs have been left unattended include the snipping off of a vital lock of hair, or the pouring of glue over a carefully combed coat. Such actions do no lasting harm to the dogs but effectively ruin their chances of winning. More

callous, but extremely rare, actions include deliberately treading on a rival dog's foot to make it limp, or feeding it an unpleasant 'titbit', so that it is feeling sick at the very moment when it should be standing proud and erect. Sometimes an owner has been accused of illegally dyeing the hair of a dog to improve its looks, but in a famous case recently the owner counter-claimed that someone else had applied the dye to discredit her.

The professional handler must be alert to all these tricks and constantly on the watch for foul play. But such incidents are so uncommon that they do not really constitute a major problem, despite attempts by the popular press to exaggerate the 'viciousness' of the competition that takes place at major shows. Michael Coad admits that there is a great deal of bitchiness, but most of this is good-humoured and even at its worst it is usually little more than hot air.

The real problems for professional handlers are of a different kind altogether. They concern the handlers' own emotions. For, all too often, they become deeply attached to the show dogs in their care and find it a tremendous wrench when the day comes for the animals to be returned to their proud owners. They may be professionals, but their feelings differ little from those of the dog show amateurs around them.

42

The Dog with the Golden Nose

His official title is Airdog Diesel Number 11134. But to his young handler, Donna Lloyd, this friendly, rather submissive, wall-eyed Cocker spaniel is known simply as Diesel. His submissiveness is due to the fact that he was ill-treated by his previous owners, but Donna is making up for this by giving him extra care and loving attention. In his new role in life, as a sniffer dog detecting drugs at Birmingham Airport, he deserves all the praise being lavished on him, for he has proved invaluable to the Customs authorities in their battle against the drug smugglers.

Only the week before we met him, he had sniffed out a batch of cannabis in a suitcase, helping to unmask yet another smuggler. He had detected the drug successfully, despite the fact that it had been sealed in a perfume-soaked envelope inside the case. We asked Donna whether attempts to screen the scent of the drugs by using other powerful odours ever worked. To our surprise, she replied that wrapping them in strong-smelling substances, far from decreasing the smell of the drugs for the dog, actually makes them easier to detect. It seems as if the perfume 'screen' switches on the dog's nose even more acutely in some way, making it a much simpler task to find the offending packet of drugs. Dogs do not confuse different smells, even when they occur close together. The canine nose is much too sensitive for that.

If it is so sensitive, it occurred to us that some villains might try to find a chemical substance that actively repelled the dogs by assailing their noses with odours so harsh and offensive that the dogs would refuse to approach the suitcase in question, drugs or no drugs. It was pointed out to us that if a sniffer dog was seen backing away from a suitcase or a package, this would be just as good a clue that something was amiss. Yes, some powerful repellents had been tried, but it had still been easy to find the drugs hidden inside the stench by watching for unusual reactions on the part of the dogs.

As a result of their amazing sense of smell, Diesel and the other sniffer dogs have uncovered countless drug hoards, with a total value running into millions. They have proved superior to any human device for drug detecting and are now respected members of the team that is fighting drug abuse in Britain and elsewhere in the world.

What makes them so efficient? To start with there is the amazing complexity of their nasal cavities, inside which there are no fewer than 220 million smell-sensitive cells. The human nose contains only a fraction of this number of cells and by comparison we are almost 'smell-blind'. At their worst, dogs are a hundred times

Desmond puts our challenge to customs officer Donna Lloyd and Airdog Diesel 11134

The hunt is on – somewhere in the pile is a consignment of cannabis

The drugs are sealed in plastic, wrapped in cardboard and hidden in a mailbag

better at odour-detection than we are, and at their best they are said to be a hundred million times better. So up against little Diesel the drug pedlars have no hope.

Donna Lloyd and her colleagues in the Customs and Excise Drug Squad staged a demonstration to convince us of Diesel's prowess. A batch of cannabis was sealed inside a heavy plastic package. The seal was so perfect that, putting a human nose close to the surface of the

plastic and inhaling deeply, it was not possible to detect even the slightest odour from inside. This package was then placed inside a cardboard box and heavy adhesive tape was wrapped around the lid. The box was then put at the bottom of a thick plastic mailbag. The mailbag was then hidden in the middle of a pile of about forty similar mailbags. Would Diesel be able to locate the one which contained the drugs?

Diesel hauls out the bag

Another smuggler thwarted by the Dog with the Golden Nose

44

Donna crouched down beside the dog and fitted a special kind of cloth harness. This acted as a signal, telling Diesel that he was now on duty. He immediately started straining to get to work and Donna had to take him quickly to where the huge pile of bags was heaped up in a corner of the baggage-transfer zone of Birmingham International Airport. As soon as she removed his lead he was off and running, leaping up on to the pile of mailbags, sniffing eagerly this way and that. In a frenzy of excitement he plunged down into the middle of the heap and then started tugging and struggling back out again, clutching a bag in his teeth. The thrill of finding something made him highly possessive. When Donna picked up the bag he clung on tightly as though his very life depended upon it. Swinging the bag round and round, Donna gave him an aerial roundabout ride until, at last, he was prepared to give up his prize. The bag was then opened and the contents revealed. Diesel had triumphed again.

How is such a dog trained? The answer, said Donna, is to make use of the animal's natural hunting urges. The hidden drugs are the 'prey'. All the trainer has to do is to divert the natural hunting energies in the direction of a new kind of 'victim'. The appeal of the odour of a rabbit or a hare has to be replaced by the new appeal of the strange odour of illicit drugs. Diesel is trained to search for cannabis, cocaine, heroin and amphetamines, but nothing else. During the training process, dummies impregnated with these specific drugs are employed and the dogs are heavily rewarded with praise and cuddles when they detect the right dummy. As Donna says, with dogs, love is the only reward you need to offer.

To become fully qualified for narcotic duty, Donna and Diesel had to go through an intensive fifteen-week course together, learning to narrow down the animal's search targets to just the four drugs on its 'hit list'. Once the dog has

Sniffer dogs like Diesel have uncovered drug hoards worth millions of pounds

become an expert at detection it immediately becomes a security risk and very special care has to be taken of it. Donna would love to take Diesel home with her at night, but that is not possible. If the drug-smugglers followed her home they could easily kill the dog and destroy the highly-trained golden nose. So, much as she hates it, Donna has to part from Diesel each evening so that he can be transported, along with his sniffer companions, to specially-protected, high-security kennels inside a well-guarded RAF base. With a dog as vital to the war against drugs as Diesel, you cannot take any chances.

Roadshow Faces

The Man they call 'Mr Snake'

Mark O'Shea loves snakes. He is obsessed with them. Describing himself as a Herpetologist/Adventurer, he devotes most of his time to studying snakes in the wild, catching them and giving talks and lectures about them. Everywhere he goes he tries his hardest to convince people that snakes are beautiful, fascinating

Mark O'Shea introduces Desmond to some of his favourite snakes

creatures that deserve our respect and attention. But it is an uphill task, for many people have a deep-seated hatred of serpents that is difficult to overcome.

This hatred seems easy to understand. Snakes are, after all, venomous and therefore highly dangerous animals. So it is perfectly logical for us to fear them. Yes and no. *Some* snakes are lethal, it is true, and great caution is required when dealing with them. But they are in the minority. Of the three thousand species of snakes alive today, fewer than three hundred have a lethal bite. So there are literally thousands of species of harmless snakes out there in the undergrowth that are needlessly subjected to human persecution. And the dangerous ones are far less of a hazard than popular legend would have you believe. In reality they will go to great lengths to avoid contact with humans. They need their precious venom to incapacitate their prey before feeding and can ill-afford to waste it on inedible people. They will only attack human beings as a very last resort when cornered or maltreated in some way.

The truth is that our fear of snakes is beyond reason. It is an irrational phobia that exists even in countries like Britain, where people exploring the countryside are statistically more likely to be struck by lightning than killed by the little European viper. Even the very rare deaths that have occurred have probably been due to panic, shock and improper treatment rather than to the venom itself. The bite of our British viper is not much worse than the sting of a large wasp or bee, but such is the terror that a snake-bite creates that the patient is vulnerable to over-reaction. All kinds of horrific treatments are applied, including lacerating the bitten flesh and cauterizing the wound. These only make matters much worse, increasing shock and causing infection. If the patient were simply kept calm and left in peace he would soon recover.

Mark O'Shea has encountered similar over-reaction in the Far East. When he was in Papua New Guinea, the local Area Forest Officer was bitten by a venomous snake and was immediately rushed to a nearby village to be given the traditional treatment of bleeding, which

So Mark's attempts to educate people and make them less fearful of snakes may easily save lives, on those rare occasions when, for example, visitors to the tropics accidentally tread on a venomous snake and get bitten. The less they panic, the less is the chance that they will die.

Because of his fascination for snakes, Mark has been given many nicknames in different parts of the world. In Honduras he is known as *Señor Culebra* (Mr Snake); in Borneo he is called *Baya Crocodile* (King of the River); and in Papua New Guinea *Giaga Tauna* (The Snakeman). To one of his expedition leaders, John Blashford-Snell, he was known affectionately as 'that lunatic', because of the apparently crazy risks he took when handling snakes. But Mark's knowledge and understanding of these reptiles has so far always protected him. Even so, there have been a few close shaves, like the time he passed his hand over the eyes of a seemingly dead snake to check if there was any pupil reaction. The snake, its back broken by frightened villagers, responded by making one last, desperate strike, and its venom-bearing fangs brushed against his skin. If the dying snake had had just a fraction more energy, Mark would have been in serious trouble. That, as he said, was a little too close for comfort, even for him.

was (falsely) believed to let out the poison. First his legs were cut open, then his arms, chest and scalp, and the poor man promptly bled to death, thereby reinforcing the belief that a snake-bite is always lethal.

An even more bizarre death occurred in India, where a man was climbing a barbed-wire fence. He felt the strike of a snake's fangs against his leg, looked down and saw a huge cobra slithering away. Examining his leg, his worst fears were realized – there were the puncture marks where the fangs had gone in. Within half an hour he was dead, but the post-mortem examination revealed that it had been the barbed wire, not the cobra, that had punctured his leg. He had died not of a snake bite, but of terror. If the shock reaction can kill when there is no venom present at all, it is easy to understand how a little venom, capable of causing a nasty swelling, can easily lead to a quite unnecessary death, simply through shock and fear.

The Dog that waited Forever

In 1923 a puppy was born in Japan on the island of Honshu and given to a Tokyo professor called Eizaburo Ueno. It was a member of the large breed of hunting dog that is usually referred to as the national dog of Japan, the Akita. The professor had wanted an Akita dog of his own for ages and was delighted with the young pup, which he called Hachi-Ko. He lived on the outskirts of Tokyo in a suburban area called Shibuya and, although he could not take his new pet with him to the city, he always allowed it to walk with him to the nearby

Mike Window introduces Sarah to the Akita

Shibuya Station to see him off in the morning. When he arrived back on the evening train, the dog was always there waiting for him, to enjoy the return walk with his master.

When Hachi was about eighteen months old, in 1925, he went to the station to meet the evening train as usual, but his master was not on it. It was impossible to make the animal understand what had happened, that the professor had suffered a sudden stroke at work and had died at the University. The dog had already made about five hundred evening trips to meet his master and the habit had become completely fixed. Attempts to dissuade him from making a useless journey the following evening were to no avail. Relatives who looked after the dog had no choice but to allow him to set off each afternoon and then wait for the early evening train to arrive, only to be disappointed once again.

Up to this point the story is not so unusual. Many a dog waits for a missing master or mistress who has suddenly and inexplicably vanished from its life. But Hachi took the business of loyalty to an almost unbelievable extreme. He continued to visit the station every day of his life until he himself died, in his twelfth year, in 1934. This means that he repeated his vigil more than three thousand times, despite endless disappointments.

It is little wonder that the Japanese see the Akita breed as a symbol of lasting loyalty and devotion. A statue was erected in memory of Hachi-Ko on the spot where he had waited every afternoon, and this statue can be seen at Shibuya Station to this day.

The Akita breed can be traced back to the seventeenth century, when it was used primarily as a hunting dog, pursuing wild boar, deer and even bear. It was the Japanese equivalent of the Chinese Chow Chow, to which it bears some resemblance. Like the Chow, it was the heavy-duty work dog of its country and when it was not hunting it was active in guarding, and was even used for pulling heavy loads. Local dog-fight organizers also employed its strength in the savagely cruel contests which were popular at this time.

By the end of the Second World War, the

The national dog of Japan is increasingly popular in the show-ring of Britain and the United States

Akita had become almost extinct and its export was forbidden in an attempt to protect the breed. But American servicemen, impressed by the dog's character and efficiency as a guard animal, brought a few back to the United States with them, despite the regulations. These formed the basis of the American Akita population and the breed has since become increasingly popular as a show dog.

We asked Mike Window, a British breeder of Akitas, who owns seven of these impressive dogs, when they first arrived in Britain and he explained that, although the first came in the 1930s and several more followed after the war, they were not fully established here as a breeding population until the 1980s, when his partner Marion imported some from the United States. Today there are approximately 350 of these powerful animals in Britain and, as in the United States, their popularity is increasing.

In personality the Akita is described as being 'steady, bold and resolute' and Mike emphasized that it is not a dog for the casual owner. It requires expert handling but, providing it is cared for by someone with experience of a large, tough-minded dog, it can be enormously re-warding. And despite its fearsome reputation, Mike insists that, 'My dogs are wonderful with children and love being petted.'

One person who would certainly have agreed with him was the late Helen Keller, the remarkable American social worker and lecturer who, despite being deaf and blind, developed a career as a globe-trotting campaigner and public speaker. She first visited Japan in 1937, where she had engagements in no fewer than thirty-nine cities. In Tokyo she learned of the amazing devotion of Hachi-Ko to his master and said how much she wished to have an Akita of her own. When she arrived in the city of Akita itself she was presented with a puppy by the local police department and took it back to the United States with her – the first Akita ever seen there. Sadly the dog lived for only a few months, but a second one was sent to Helen Keller in New York in 1939 and it was this one, Kenzan-Go, which was to make the first real impact on American dog enthusiasts. Even today, the United States is the most Akita-conscious country outside Japan itself, but if Mike Window has anything to do with it Britain will soon be catching up.

51

Have Dog-Breeders gone Too Far?

Mike Stockman is the Chairman of the Breed Standards Committee of the august Kennel Club, the governing body for all the major British dog shows. It is his task to examine closely the precise standards that are laid down for each breed to see if there is any need for modification or improvement. In this role he wears two hats – his traditional Kennel Club hat that requires him to stick to the old, well-established descriptions of breeds, and, since he is a qualified veterinary surgeon, his scientific Vet's hat that makes him criticize some of the extreme forms of exaggeration that have become the 'norm' for certain pedigree dogs.

The Dachshund

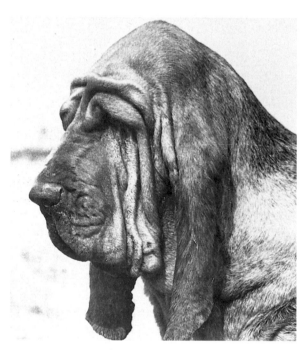

The Bloodhound

As a vet he insists that each breed should be able to breathe normally, reproduce normally and walk normally, fitting into natural conditions as a well-balanced animal. He also stresses that, in examining the problems of pedigree dogs, one should not over-emphasize the difficulties, as some critics have done. There are over 150 different breeds recognized by the Kennel Club and of these, he says, only fifteen to twenty have any features which give cause

for alarm. So the vast majority of pedigree dogs are perfectly healthy, physically well-adjusted animals, despite their sometimes bizarre appearance.

In each of the small number of troublesome breeds, there is usually only one special feature that creates problems and this can easily be put right by careful selective breeding without upsetting other aspects of the breed. The modern Bloodhound, for example, has an excellent

The Pekinese

body except for its eyes, which droop so much that they sometimes require surgical attention. The Dachshund has had its body length increased and increased by selective breeding until it is now at risk from back ailments such as slipped discs. And the flat-faced dogs such as the Pekinese and the Bulldog suffer from breathing problems. Both these last breeds could be selectively bred to have slightly longer faces, which would improve their respiration without robbing them of their special appeal. All that is needed in these different cases is a very slight move away from the highly exaggerated form that is at present in favour. For this reason the Kennel Club is trying to make its Breed Standards a little more flexible in the hope that breeders will see the advantages of pulling back from the more extreme refinements.

It is important that these steps should be taken because it is these few difficult breeds that are always held up by critics as representing the 'decadence' of pedigree dogs. They represent only a small minority but, because of them, the whole of the show dog world comes under fire as being damagingly artificial. The dog breeders are said to be more interested in their dogs' beauty than their comfort. And yet the vast majority of pedigree dogs are as tough, resilient, hardy and happy as any streetwise mongrel bursting with hybrid vigour. It is vital that we keep a sense of proportion and, with incisive men like Mike Stockman in charge of the Breed Standards situation, the future looks bright. Under the enlightened guidance of its chairman, John MacDougall, the Kennel Club is determined to be positive and up-to-date in its thinking. It is obviously in good hands.

The Bulldog

The Dog with a Novel Name

The only breed of dog to take its name from a character in a novel is the remarkable little Dandie Dinmont. It acquired this title, courtesy of Sir Walter Scott, at the beginning of the nineteenth century, but as a breed it had been known for at least a hundred years before that. It started life in the Border country between England and Scotland as a gypsy mongrel. Nobody knows exactly which terriers were its forerunners, but everyone enjoys hazarding a guess. The most likely is the Skye terrier, but others that are considered as ancestral to the

There are only about 3,000 Dandie Dinmonts in the world

breed include the Scottie, the Bedlington, the Cairn and the Border terrier. There has even been mention of the Otterhound and the Basset-hound, presumably to explain the presence of drooping ears. The truth is that we will never know the precise origin of the breed, but we do know the role it has played. It was bred as a very short-legged, long-bodied ratter and general vermin-destroyer, that attacked not only rats but also mice, rabbits, martens, badgers, otters and foxes. Despite its soulful eyes and innocent-looking face, it was said to be one of the fiercest and most tenacious attackers. Once it had sunk its teeth into a quarry's hind leg, it was claimed that, even if its victim was a dragon or a giant, it would never let go and had no fear whatsoever.

These ferocious little dogs with angelic expressions were given many names by their eighteenth-century owners. In fact they were not really given a breed name as such, but rather a series of local or family nicknames. One Border farmer called James Davidson had six of these terriers which he had named 'Auld Pepper and Auld Mustard, Young Pepper and Young Mustard, and Little Pepper and Little Mustard'. Sir Walter Scott, amused by this strange way of naming dogs by their colour and age, incorporated them and their owner into his 1814 novel *Guy Mannering*. He changed the name of the farmer to Dandie Dinmont and described the dogs as 'Dandie Dinmont's Pepper and Mustard terriers'. In the novel he has the farmer say that he sets his terriers after 'rottens, stots, weasels, tods, brocks and fumarts' (being local names for rats, stoats, weasels, foxes, badgers and polecats) and that 'now they fear nothing that ever came with a hairy skin on't.'

The success of this novel was such that it made the little terriers famous and their popularity soared. By about 1820 they had come to be called Dandie Dinmont terriers, after their fictitious owner, and were well-established as a new breed. When the Kennel Club was formed later in the century, they were one of the first three breeds (along with the Bulldog and the Bedlington) ever registered there and the Dandie Dinmont Terrier Club of 1875 is one of

Falla greets Sir Hector every time he returns north from Westminster: she doesn't bark, but just squeals and sings and 'nearly kills him with love'. Lady Munro says that, in her opinion, one of the breed's good qualities is that the animals are never bad-tempered. If upset, they react in a different way: 'They're tremendous characters. If they don't like what you say, they go into a Dandie huff, just like a naughty child that has been ticked off. Falla turns her back on me, won't eat her food and sulks for up to a day. It's dreadful. I practically have to go down on both arthritic knees and beg for forgiveness.' Clearly a most interesting dog, but one with a mind of its own.

The Munros with their large family of Dandie Dinmonts

the three oldest canine breed clubs in the world. Its patron today is the great-great-great-granddaughter of Sir Walter Scott. But despite this long history and the great loyalty of the 'DD' enthusiasts, the breed has never been among the top favourites of the present century. Given their extraordinary appearance and their fascinating personalities this is rather surprising, but the enthusiasts are far from worried. They prefer the breed to remain exclusive and unexploited.

An early author remarked that, 'To those who desire to slobber over a pet and invite it to come to mother's arms the Dandie is not recommended; it has a satiric attitude to the sentimental.' But he went on to sing its praises as a charmingly independent companion with a fascinating personality, its only fault being that, 'it resents quietly and firmly interference in its plans'. It makes up for this, however, by being fond of children and other dogs and extremely adaptable to any kind of living environment - from a tent to a castle.

When we visited the breed's homelands at Dumfries we spoke to the local M.P. Sir Hector Munro and his wife, who have kept and bred Dandie Dinmonts for twenty years. Lady Munro described the way in which their bitch

The Animal Cure

Enter most wards in hospitals dedicated to the care of the elderly and infirm and you enter a world of quiet, neat efficiency. But look around – it is also a world of quiet, neat monotony. The old people occupying these wards have little excitement, few surprises and hardly any direct contact with the natural world. The vacant expressions and unfocused stares that confront you are often no more than a form of protection from the bleak predictability of life. In an act of self-preservation the old people turn in on themselves and feed off their memories.

Matron Mary Curran at Heathcote Hospital in Leamington Spa is a creative rebel who refused to accept this situation and took highly unconventional steps to alter it. Seeing how withdrawn her elderly patients had become, she decided to bring some life into her wards, literally, in the shape of domestic animals. First she tried a cat. The old people loved it, but the staff were unhappy and removed it. So she went

Stroking animals can be therapeutic

to the Guide Dog Association and asked them for any rejects they might have. This time, even the staff enjoyed the additions to the wards and began to see the advantages of a livelier atmosphere. As Mary Curran expressed it, the animals helped to put the emphasis back on 'the life left in years, rather than the years left in life'. Boring days became eventful days, full of unpredictable moments and touching encounters – in both senses of the word 'touching'.

The hospital menagerie, wandering freely about the wards and corridors, grew to four dogs and five cats, but more was to come. Three donkeys were added. Originally these were obtained to try and persuade some of the older people out into the sunshine. But the donkeys had other ideas. Amazingly, they enjoyed entering the wards and trotting calmly up and down, being patted here, stroked there. Vacant stares and unfocused eyes were becoming more and more rarely observed by the staff. Lined old faces were on the look-out, watching for the next surprise. What would pop up next, and where, and when? Monotony was magically banished by the mere presence of these friendly animals. The matron had transformed a dull institution into a cheerful, friendly home.

One elderly woman, after having her leg amputated, did not want to go on living. She had had enough. But Mary Curran soon found a way of removing her depression. She introduced tame goats into the ward and supplied the old lady with bottles of milk with which to feed them every day. The goats were greedily grateful and the patient found herself eagerly awaiting each of their visits. Life had some meaning once again.

A dog called Sheba delighted in delivering the daily newspaper to an elderly man suffering from Parkinson's disease. It added one more pleasant anticipation to the rhythm of the day.

The medical authorities were somewhat taken aback by this unconventional approach to medical care – curing boredom with animals. Some were concerned about questions of hygiene. The matron vigorously and quite rightly rejects all such criticism. She argues that if excessive regard for hygiene leads to mental sterility in her patients then it is a

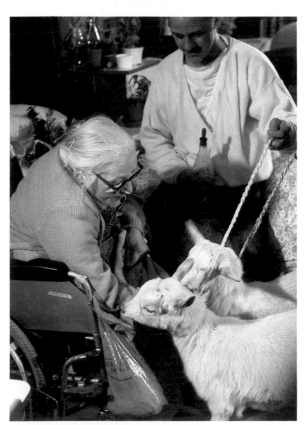

Animals bring a new zest for life to the wards of Heathcote Hospital in Leamington Spa

serious danger to their quality of life. Furthermore, she claims that, properly looked after and managed, the animals are *not* unhygienic in the wards. The larger animals have excellent living quarters in the hospital grounds and the staff have become completely converted to this more exciting way of looking after people in their final years.

We came away from Heathcote Hospital marvelling at the intelligence and imagination of matron Mary Curran. We also came away puzzling at the astonishing *lack* of imagination in so many other hospitals for the elderly and sick, hospitals where there seems to be an acceptance of an almost Victorian routine of dull rituals and boringly repetitive procedures. We may have made great advances in pharmaceutics and surgery in recent years, but we still have a lot to learn from people like Mary Curran when it comes to the equally important matter of caring about the lifestyle of the extremely elderly and infirm.

A friendly donkey in the ward makes an ass of rigid traditions.

The Naked Dog

The weirdest-looking breed at any modern dog show is undoubtedly the little Chinese Crested dog. Its strange, usually blotched or spotted, skin is completely naked except for a tuft of hair at the end of the tail, tufts between the toes and a great, fluffy crest on top of the head. This remarkable appearance fascinates people at first glance, but then, after they have studied it for a while, they either fall in love with it or come to loathe it as being freakish. Certainly it makes the animal look very un-doglike, and it is understandable that those who enjoy long walks over winter fields with their canine companions are going to frown on this 'hot-house' creation. But for others, who favour the exotic and the unusual, it is a breed with great appeal.

It is also a breed shrouded in mystery and contradiction. Every authority admits that its origin is unknown, but then proceeds to describe the most likely way in which it has come down to us. Unfortunately this leaves us with a number of totally different histories for the breed and it is hard to choose between them. What seems to have happened is that hairless dogs have cropped up from time to time in widely separate parts of the world and these isolated individuals have been confused with one another, relationships between them being mistakenly imagined.

We know, for instance, that there have been naked or hairless breeds in North Africa, Turkey, Manchuria, China, South America and Mexico, and it has been assumed that one of these countries was the original source from which the carefully-bred offspring were exported to the others. This is not likely. A more probable explanation is that genes for hairlessness have arisen independently in these different regions and have produced similar dogs in each place, without any export/import trade being involved. It is even doubtful that the breed we now call the Chinese Crested dog has any connection whatever with China.

The African specimens have been named as the Abyssinian Hairless dog, the African Sand dog, the Egyptian Hairless dog and the Barbary dog. Because of their oddity these animals were brought first to zoos rather than to more homely firesides. London Zoo records that the

The remarkable Chinese Crested dog

first Egyptian Hairless dog arrived there in 1833 and the first Barbary dog in 1839. They died without starting new lines of pedigree dogs.

The Turkish Naked dog, known as early as 1791, did not fare well either. Said to be like a hairless, flat-faced version of the Italian greyhound, it was found to be extremely delicate in the British climate. Some authorities believe that it was nevertheless the ancestor of the Chinese Crested dog. Another strong candidate for such a role is a remarkable Manchurian naked dog, imported into the United States after the Second World War. It was featured in *Life* magazine, and photographs reveal that it had a spotted skin and a crest of white hair.

Another scenario has Chinese traders bringing the hairless dog from China to South and Central America in earlier centuries – some say as early as the sixth or seventh centuries – and trading it there with the local populations. This may have happened, but a visit to the National Museum in Mexico throws some doubt on the idea. There, in the section dealing with ancient Tlatilco, is a small figurine from the second millennium B.C., which shows a woman hugging and kissing a tiny prick-eared dog with bulging eyes. It seems likely that today's Mexican Hairless dogs therefore have a much longer local history than most people imagine. It is even possible that the ancient civilizations of the Americas sent *their* naked dogs to China, rather than the other way around.

We may never know the truth about where the Chinese Crested dog came from originally, but we do know something about the uses to which hairless dogs have been put. The Peruvian Inca Moonflower dog and the Mexican Xoloitzcuintli were both employed as hot-water bottles on cold nights, the naked skin always feeling very hot to the touch. They were also fattened as food and many of the Colima pottery figurines from north-west Mexico show an extremely rotund 'melon-shaped' dog that would clearly have provided a juicy meal when times were hard.

Some of these pre-Columbian dogs were known as Temple dogs, because they were thought to be useful as guides for the souls of the deceased journeying to the afterlife. Remains of these dogs have been found in tombs dating back to as early as 1400 B.C., suggesting that they may have been sacrificed at the funeral rites so that they could more promptly accompany their masters to the other world.

It may have been simply their oddity that made them suitable candidates for these sacred duties, but there is an additional factor that may have been important. For the naked breeds are in one sense more human because, like us, they have lost their thick coat of fur. The Chinese Crested dog, in particular, has the curious human-like combination of a naked body with a hairy head. Perhaps this similarity with people is also the reason why it was thought to have magical healing powers. In 1928 a specimen arriving in London was

advertized as a 'Fever dog', because it was claimed that merely to touch its skin would cure a human fever. Holding naked dogs close to the body was widely believed to be a remedy for a whole variety of ailments and it is surprising that, with this in their favour, such dogs did not become more popular.

In fact, the first signs of interest in the 1920s and 1930s quickly faded and the naked dog disappeared altogether. Then after another twenty years or so it reappeared and in 1965 the British breed club for the Chinese Crested dog was formed, to be followed in 1975 by the American club. Now at last there is a growing band of supporters for these bizarre little animals and they appear to be firmly established for the future.

We spoke to Dick Dickinson, the President of the Chinese Crested Dog Society of America, and asked him why he thought the appeal of the breed was growing. He explained that, once you overcome the dog's strange appearance, it is an extremely attractive breed to hold in your hands, its skin being warm and smooth to the touch, 'just like picking up a baby'.

Mirrie Cardew, another Chinese Crested dog expert we met on our travels, who has just written a book called *A Chinese Crested Dog for Me*, sums up her own enthusiasm for the breed in the following way: 'He is different. He has meticulous habits. He is a dog whose skin changes with the seasons. He lacks doggy smell. He washes himself like a cat. He has a great sense of humour. He is an excellent house dog and guard. He is an ideal size. He is a great conversation piece.' With friends like this, the extraordinary breed may well be seen much more in the years ahead.

59

The Puppy in a Cat's Body

Of all pedigrees, few are as romantic as that of the Birman cat. In cat-breeding terms, the Birman is an exotic semi-longhaired variety; according to Burmese tradition, it is much more colourful than that.

High on the slopes of Mount Lugh, in western Burma, sat a temple called Lao Tsun. There, centuries ago, the Kittah priests worshipped the goddess Tsun-Kyun-Kse, to whose care the transmigration of souls was entrusted. The figure of the goddess was golden and her eyes were a brilliant sapphire blue. Reflecting their faith in reincarnation, the priests kept a hundred pure white cats with yellow eyes, for they believed that after death the soul of a priest would enter the body of a cat. There it would rest until the cat passed away, and the human soul was set free to enter paradise. Should anyone kill or harm a sacred cat, the punishment was that his soul should wander in endless torment throughout eternity.

The chief priest, Mun-Ha, formed a deep attachment to a cat called Sinh, who was always by his side. One night, in the midnight

The white-footed Birman cat

hour, Mun-Ha knelt in silent worship at the feet of the goddess. A band of marauding Thai bandits suddenly assaulted the temple and, before the terrified gaze of his fellow priests, Mun-Ha was struck down as he prayed to his goddess for deliverance. In silent grief, the faithful Sinh placed his paws on the head of his dying master. As the transmigration of souls took place, a miracle occurred. A golden glow shone from the figure of the goddess and then slowly moved over the cat, changing its coat to a warm golden hue. As the cat gazed into the face of the goddess, his yellow eyes became a brilliant sapphire blue to match her own. At the same time, Sinh's nose, ears, legs and tail darkened to the colour of the earth while his feet, resting on the silvery head of his master, remained white as a symbol of purity.

Meanwhile the temple priests were huddled together, in mortal fear of the barbarians. As

Sinh turned from the goddess to look at them with commanding eyes, their courage soared and they repelled the invaders. Only then did they discover that each of the other ninety-nine temple cats had undergone the same transformation as the faithful Sinh.

Sinh remained with his dead master for seven days and nights, refusing food and water until he too eventually died. As he did so he allowed the soul of his master to enter the eternal paradise of Song Hio.

This was the accepted legend at the beginning of the twentieth century when the Burmese temple was raided again. It was saved once more, this time with the help of two Europeans, Major Gordon Russell and Monsieur Auguste Pavie. A few years later the two men were living in France when the temple priests sent them two of the sacred cats as a gift. The male died en route but the female survived and proved to be with kitten. Her litter thrived and by 1925 the Birman had become a recognized breed in France. Although they almost became extinct during the Second World War, a few dedicated breeders nursed them through the German occupation. By 1965 they were being imported into Britain, where their popularity continues to grow.

The breeder and judge David Redtfeldt told us he finds them wonderfully affectionate – 'like puppy dogs in cat's bodies' – with none of the independent streak normally associated with cats. He finds they have a need to be with people: his own even visits him in the bath.

Cat experts were fascinated in 1960 when a pair of Tibetan temple kittens was sent to the United States. Their colouring and coat pattern were identical with the Birman's. Their history seemed to be similar too. A long time ago, it appeared, they had shared a common ancestry.

The Appeal of the Sausage Dog

Alan Sharman is a retired banker who has not taken a holiday for twenty-five years. The reason is simple: his dogs come first. His whole life now revolves around his champion Dachshunds, and he even takes them to bed with him. He claims that they make the best bed-warmers he has ever had and that they are far less trouble than a wife. In fact, he is prepared to admit that he prefers his dogs to people.

Like so many specialist dog breeders he has become a fanatical enthusiast where his breed is concerned and fiercely protective of them. Heaven help any prospective buyer who dares to ask him whether one of his puppies will make a suitable pet. His reaction is always to question whether the buyer will make a suitable owner. To ensure this, he interrogates the unfortunate person and, if he does not measure up to the high standards Alan requires, he is sent packing. One man who was rejected after questioning, because Alan did not like his little daughter, became so angry that he physically attacked Alan, demanding that he part with one of his prize puppies. Even though he was knocked to the ground, Alan refused to capitulate and eventually had to give the man money to get rid of him.

What is it about this little dog that arouses such strong passions and creates such powerful feelings of loyalty? The breed was originally developed in Germany as a terrier for following badgers underground and attacking them there. The name 'Dachshund' is German for 'badger dog', but it was mistranslated in the last century as 'badger hound' and the dogs were first shown as 'German badger hounds'. Inevitably, this led to their being classed with the other hounds instead of with the terriers. When the experts reverted to the German title, the hound classification remained and to this day the diminutive 'sausage dog' has been grouped together with the bigger hounds.

Dachshund enthusiasts have done little to alter this state of affairs because they argue that the Dachshunds have a more dignified, hound-like personality than the other terriers. Terrier owners would not agree with this, but it has to be said that if you look at a photograph of a Dachshund and place your hand over its legs, its upper region does look remarkably like that of a large hound. The argument will no doubt continue for many years.

The first Dachshunds to come to Britain were privileged pets, given by Prince Edward of Saxe-Weimar to the Prince Consort around 1840. They were kept at Windsor and quickly became favourites with Queen Victoria. At this date in their history they were more active working dogs, with shorter bodies and longer legs than the present-day pedigree specimens. Even so, they were very low-slung and were

Alan Sharman with one of his Dachshunds

infant and have the clumsiness of gait that makes them seem rather babyish. They cannot go bounding off like long-legged dogs. This gives them a vulnerability that arouses very strong protective feelings from their owners.

This basic contradiction – the spirit of a great hound coupled with the body of a small puppy – is the secret of the breed's unique appeal. It makes the animal into a proud, plucky little child that stimulates the maternal (or paternal) reactions of those who care for them. The words the enthusiasts use to describe the personality of the Dachshund are revealing: mischievous, affectionate, tough, stubborn, good-humoured, clever, lively and intelligent – all the qualities of the perfect child-companion. But it should be added that this is in no way a criticism of the attitudes of those devoted dog owners. All our pet-keeping has a strong element of transformed parental care and there is no harm in that.

clearly highly specialized for going to earth.

In 1881 the Dachshund Club was formed and breeders set about 'improving' the shape of the animal. This entailed selecting for longer backs and even shorter legs, until the underside of the dog nearly brushed the ground as it walked. As far as the owners and breeders were concerned this was an advance, because it increased the 'comical' qualities of the dog. If the Dachshunds themselves could have been consulted they might not have agreed. It reduced their ability to walk and run fast and it rendered them vulnerable to backaches and slipped discs, especially if they became a little overweight.

Sadly these exaggerations were soon enshrined as a traditional part of the breed standards at dog shows and there was little hope of seeing them reversed. If they made the dogs less healthy, then why did those who cared so much for these dogs insist on keeping the 'advanced' body shape? The answer is simple. As far as the dogs themselves are concerned, they see themselves as great, bold hounds and act accordingly. They have a deep bark for such a small dog and the spirit of a breed three times their height. This combination gives them the air of bravery and courage that Dachshund owners so often refer to. It fosters admiration. At the same time, they are not much bigger than a human

The Fast Ladies of Rotten Row

Anyone seeking the origin of the phrase 'fast ladies' might find an interesting answer in the most famous bridleway in the world, Rotten Row, which runs like a breath of country air through Hyde Park in the very heart of London. In its fashionable prime, around the middle of the nineteenth century, the society of the time laid down firm rules of etiquette for conduct in the Row. Galloping was frowned upon and even the extended trot was regarded with disfavour. Most important of all, no lady was expected to go out riding without a gentleman to escort her and see that she remained safe.

There were of course a few flighty ladies who flouted the conventions and provoked indignant letters to the newspapers. They were described by the Victorians (with consummate hypocrisy) as the 'pretty horsebreakers'. In fact they were young women of outstanding riding ability who were employed by London dealers and riding academies to school and finish their horses and to display their mettle to potential customers in the park. Since some of the 'pretty horsebreakers' were as spirited as their steeds and distinctly ahead of their time, they were often labelled as notorious ladies.

For at least three hundred years Rotten Row has been part of the royal parks that Pitt the Elder once described as the lungs of London. To ride along it today at dawn in summer is to consort with the ghosts of some of the most illustrious figures in English history. Indeed Rotten Row's prominence in the story of horsemanship is without parallel. It was first laid down in the winter of 1689–90 under the

The oldest bridleway in the world, Rotten Row

around the Park with several hundred horses. Today only three stables are left on lease, with fewer than fifty horses among them. The Kennedy children learned to ride here on horses hired from the stables of Lilo Blum. Her horses have been ridden by such celebrities as Zsa Zsa Gabor and Raquel Welch, Mohammed Ali and the occasional Arab millionaire. On a canter before going to their offices, West End secretaries may indeed share the Row with Prince and Princess Michael of Kent.

What has altered most profoundly is the value of the land in the heart of the capital. As Rotten Row prepares to celebrate its official tercentenary in 1990, its committee chairman Neil Mitchell points to the irony of insupportable costs for stabling at a time when more people than ever before are enjoying equestrian pursuits. There are around twenty-five thousand riders in and around London, yet the most densely populated metropolis in the West, Manhattan in New York, now boasts more civilian stabling than Westminster. Left to market forces, public riding in central London could end by the turn of the century.

Lilo Blum talks to Desmond

supervision of King William III's surveyor of roads and was the first thoroughfare in the kingdom to be continuously lit by lamps. Originally it was to be part of the royal carriage drive from Westminster to Kensington Palace. The name itself may come from either the French for royal route or from the English rotten, indicating the softness of its sandy surface.

It was used by a long line of monarchs right up to Victoria and George V. Yet its heyday was undoubtedly the time when the Victorian age was at its most confident. Park riding then was a crowded social event shaping conventions and styles which can be seen today. Equestrian morning dress consisted of riding overalls, swallowtail or frock coat, and the silk hat which still survives in the hack classes of some major shows. The women's liberation movement in one sense struck its first blow for freedom in Rotten Row. Small girls from early in the nineteenth century were taught to ride astride prior to going decorously side-saddle. The first ladies to defy tradition began wearing, in the 1890s, modest outfits of divided skirts or, occasionally, breeches and boots. Even so it was an unwritten rule that they reverted to side-saddle when hacking in the Park in the presence of royalty.

Now a rural island in the stream of motorized traffic which displaced the horse, Rotten Row is fundamentally unchanged. Only the numbers have altered. Once there were dozens of stables

65

The Dog that tastes like Lamb

Some years ago a rich American couple were travelling in the Far East with their pet dog. Visiting a restaurant where the waiter spoke no English, they ordered their food as best they could by pointing at the menu. Their dog was also hungry, so the woman made gestures asking the waiter to bring food for the animal as well. She did this by pointing at the dog and then towards her mouth. The waiter smiled and nodded and took the dog away. The couple assumed that the animal was to be fed in the kitchen, or outside somewhere, but the waiter had misunderstood the gestures and returned later with the dog cooked and served up as their lunch. The woman fainted and East–West relations suffered a severe setback.

The inscrutable Chow Chow

We in the West have always found it repulsive to think of a dog as a source of meat for the table, but this taboo on canine flesh has been much less common in the Far East. Even today dogs are still eaten as a special delicacy in certain oriental countries and in the past the practice was widespread. So much so that the pidgin English expression for food was the same as the local name for the edible dog: 'Chow'.

The Chow-dogs were farmed in large numbers in previous centuries but in those days were not considered to be part of Chinese *haute cuisine*. They were scorned by the upper and middle classes and were devoured only by the poorer members of society. Their flesh was said to taste like lamb and, in order to give it the correct flavour, the dogs were fed on a controlled vegetable diet. Percy Whittaker, known in the dog world affectionately as Mr Chow because he has been involved with the breed for over seventy years, told me that the very first specimens of Chow-dogs he saw in this country, freshly imported from China, could not stomach the meaty diet offered them on their arrival here. They had to be carefully weaned on to it to prevent sickness.

In old China the edible dogs were kept penned up like pigs, in dog-sties. There they were fattened up to be slaughtered by a special dog-butcher when they were between ten and twelve months old. Apparently only the legs were eaten and these were said to be extremely tender and tasty.

Their thick, furry hair was also much prized for trimming the coats of women and, in the far north of the country, whole pelts of Chow were popular means of protection against the cold. Providing farmers with food and fur was not, however, the original function of the Chow-dogs. As the heaviness of their coats and their stocky build would suggest, they were originally dogs of the far, frozen north, related no doubt to the Eskimo dogs such as the Husky, the Malamute and the Samoyed. Their first role was probably as sledge dogs. Even after they were brought south into China from the Siberian wastelands they were employed as beasts of burden, and one of the earliest representations of them, dating back to the Han dynasty, about two thousand years ago, shows them clad in a leather harness. It depicts them in a legendary role, leading the dead safely to the underworld. In real life they were more often seen pulling heavy carts, which they were expected to transport on cruelly inadequate diets.

Their impressive physical strength and endurance, which made them such excellent draught animals, was inevitably exploited in other spheres. They were fearsome guard dogs and when battles raged they were thrown into action as 'dogs of war'. Whenever the barbarian hordes living to the north of China made sweeps to the south, they brought with them large numbers of these tough, ferocious dogs, increasing the local population still further. At other times they were employed as hunting dogs, in the chase after wolves and other large and difficult prey. In this capacity they became renowned as the fiercest of breeds and, even today, the seemingly docile show-Chows have to be kept under tight control in the presence of farm stock such as sheep.

At a large dog show today, the Chow (or Chow Chow as it is called by the enthusiasts) stands out from the other dogs because of its unusual appearance, gait and personality. In appearance it looks like a lion, with its thick mane or ruff of fur surrounding its impressive face. Its expression is enigmatic and its gaze distant – another leonine quality. Its gait is stiff and stilted, quite unlike that of any other breed of dog, and with its reserved air of restrained aloofness, it seems to show far less 'body language' than other dogs. This inscrutable personality is something which appeals to Chow owners, who can often be heard saying of their dogs that they are difficult to train, but they will die for you even if they won't obey you.

A few authorities, who should have known better, have stated that the Chow is so unusual that it is not a true dog. Instead they see it as an intermediate form between a dog and a bear. Needless to say, this is pure fantasy and the Chow is 100 per cent dog. One of the reasons for this strange bear theory is, of all things, the colour of the Chow's tongue. All typical breeds of dogs today have a pink tongue and pinkish lining to the mouth. The Chow, however, has a blue-black tongue and mouth, something which it shares with the Asiatic bears. This, however, is the only close similarity between Chow and bear and is apparently no more than an accidental resemblance. (The only other breed of dog with this blue-black tongue is a close relative of the Chow, the Chinese Shar-pei.)

There is no scientific explanation for this peculiar coloration. The only suggestion on offer comes from an old Chinese fairy tale which states that, when the world was being created, only one dog was allowed to lick up all the little pieces of blue sky which fell to earth when the stars were being set in their place. That dog was the Chow and he licked so hard that it left him with a permanently blue tongue.

Roadshow Exotics

A Monarch for a Monarch

On his Gloucestershire estate, the Prince of Wales has set aside a meadow specifically for butterflies. Following closely the advice of conservationist Dr Miriam Rothschild, His Royal Highness has planted only flowers beneficial to the Painted Ladies and Monarchs of the British countryside.

It may seem rather strange to go to such lengths to accommodate insects that can always be seen fluttering around on the few sunny summer days we enjoy on this island, but when did you last see an Indian Leaf butterfly or a Large Blue? Not recently enough, according to Richard Lamb of the Stratford Butterfly Farm. The problem, he says, is progress. With

the constant encroachment of urban development on the natural countryside, butterflies, along with much other wildlife, are at increasing risk of becoming scarce or even extinct. Already in Britain, native species such as the Large Copper, Large Blue and Black-veined White have been lost and many others are known to be in great danger. A quick count among the Animals Roadshow team confirmed Richard's thesis: few of us could remember the last time we had seen more than the odd butterfly at any one time.

This is where Richard and his colleagues take up the battle. At Stratford Butterfly Farm,

as at many similar wildlife protection centres all over Britain, they are collecting and breeding those species which are at serious risk due to loss of habitat and food source. Theirs is a living collection, designed to be seen by, and to influence, as many people as possible; not just academic enthusiasts but all of us. The Stratford Farm sets out to create an awareness of the great loss we would experience if we let our countryside and wildlife diminish unchecked.

As we walked with Richard through an atmosphere alive with exotic butterflies of every colour imaginable, we were shown how, by careful planning and control, a tropical environment has been created which favours the healthy progression of the butterflies through every stage of their life cycle. Many children we saw were totally preoccupied with the caterpillars munching away on cabbage leaves, or with the frogs and amphibians to be found relaxing around the pools. Others screwed up their eyes in an attempt to distinguish the more ingeniously camouflaged insects at rest on brilliantly coloured flowers. The great eye-like markings on the underwings of the Owl butterflies are thought to imitate the eyes of lizards, snakes or owls. Other butterflies have eye-like markings at the edge of their wings which distract the attention of the enemy from the vulnerable parts of the body.

Visitors contribute to the success of the Stratford Farm precisely because, once inside, they do not constitute a threat; outside they do. There can be little doubt that the construction of the motorways that carried the Animals Roadshow team to Stratford disrupted the foodchain of most of the species inside the farm, destroying large areas of what we consider to be weeds, such as nettles, clover and dock. What is left may be contaminated with pesticides. If we continue in this way, Richard says, our children will have little natural beauty to enjoy.

Richard and his colleagues earnestly hope that what is on view in their farm will change people's attitudes, especially as the twenty thousand species of butterfly in the world have already survived so much. One species at the

farm, the Monarch, is noted for its migrations across the Atlantic, from America as far as the Scilly Isles. It would be a sad thing if it were to fly all that way and find no field and no food.

As we left the farm, an Australian Birdwing butterfly with an amazing 10-inch wingspan flew over our heads. Richard says that the next time we visit, the farm will have acquired the most aggressive butterfly in the world, the powerful *Charaxes candiope* of Uganda, which attacks people intruding into its territory.

During the Second World War, when Prince Charles's grandfather was King, Winston Churchill bred butterflies, including Monarchs, at his country estate to help him relax. But as Richard Lamb would be the first to remind us, at that time Britain was still a green and pleasant land.

71

A Dog in the Bush . . .

The Cocker spaniel is not so-called because it cocks its leg more often than other dogs, but because its special task on the hunting field was originally to flush out woodcock. It is an unusually small, compact spaniel breed, developed several hundred years ago to push its way more easily through low, dense bushes in search of its special quarry. It became immensely popular on the hunt because of its efficiency not only at flushing, but also at finding and retrieving.

In addition to being so useful in hunting, the Cocker spaniel also proved to be one of the friendliest breeds, with a good-natured, affectionate and generally fun-loving personality. Sociable, even with strangers, and obedient to its master, it was inevitably destined to become immensely popular away from the hunt as well as on it. As a companion dog it flourished in the

The Cocker spaniel – one of the most popular dogs in Britain

last century and when dog shows were started in the 1850s it soon became one of the major competitors. By 1935 it had risen to become the most popular breed of all in the pedigree dog world and it retained this number one position for the next twenty years.

The field sportsmen viewed this new-found success in the home and the show-ring with mild disgust. Cockers were now being bred for 'showy' qualities, regardless of the true character of the breed. What had been a cheerful, tireless and courageous companion on the hunt had, in their view, now deteriorated into an inbred, pampered pet which was over-emotional, hyper-sensitive and excessively nervous. They blamed this on the show breeders and on the fact that the spaniels were not being given enough field exercise, which they considered essential to their well-being. As one authority put it: 'Too many are now highly strung and excitable. Moreover, the features which are particularly admired on the show-bench, and which some breeders tend to exaggerate for that very reason, are precisely those which render the dog unsuitable for work in cover.' He goes on to lament the fact that today the Cocker spaniel, as the dog of the rough shooter, has all but vanished.

There is some truth in this view, but it is slightly biased. It is true that some pet spaniels have developed a nervous disposition, but this is really more the fault of their owners than the result of some fundamental genetic change in the breed. Spaniels need to express themselves and if they are kept in cotton wool too much will inevitably start to become frustrated and nervous. Given sufficient outlets for their great natural energy, they will remain the friendly, cheerful dogs they have always been. Their transition to fireside pets demands a great deal of them in adaptability, so before we criticize them as over-active busybodies, we would do well to remember the kind of animal we have lying on our rug. It is not a trouble-maker, it is an out-of-work hunter. A dog on the dole.

Those spaniel owners who recognize the social problem of a gundog in a gunless world and who do their best to keep their pets active and interested will know that, as a companion,

the Cocker spaniel remains to this day a most rewarding pet and a willing show dog. And these wise owners will champion their favourite breed against all criticisms. This is just as well for the modern Cockers because recently they have come under attack from a new direction. This time it is not from the old-fashioned field sportsmen, but from the veterinary world. A number of vets have noticed that cocker spaniels have been appearing more and more frequently before them, accused of sudden, inexplicable attacks on their owners. The attacks occur without provocation or warning and have several characteristic features. The spaniel's eyes become glazed and it growls at nothing in particular. From a typically friendly mood, the animal suddenly becomes intensely aggressive and bites its owner or a member of his family. Then, just as suddenly, it is its usual friendly self again, as though nothing has happened. The vets describe what occurs as being rather like a 'fit', in which the dog does not know what it is doing.

This behaviour has been dubbed the 'rage syndrome' and is thought to be a hereditary defect limited to certain colours and strains of cocker spaniel, which vets feel should be gradually eliminated from the breeding population. One records that of all Cockers brought to him for examination, 63 per cent had bitten their owners and 25 per cent had bitten children of the owning family. The veterinary profession takes this problem very seriously indeed. It is strongly opposed on this issue by many of the most experienced Cocker breeders and showers. Little love is lost between the two sides. The breeders feel that the so-called 'rage syndrome' is merely a figment of the vets' imagination and that all cases of these dogs attacking their owners are the result of the dogs not having been given enough exercise and excitement in their lives. Supporting them in this view is the observation that highly active *wild* animals, when caged in small zoo enclosures, often show 'rage', even attacking their own bodies if they are kept in solitary confinement. Such rages are not due to inbreeding, or to 'special strains' of these wild species. They are simply the intense frustration reactions of highly active animals kept in conditions of unacceptable restraint and boredom. The Cocker, bred for centuries to be tirelessly energetic on the hunt, cannot always face the 'peace and quiet' of the domestic, urban environment. Its reaction is to attack those responsible for its confinement. But they are also the loved members of its adopted 'pack'. The intensity of the conflict it feels is so unbearable that it suffers something akin to a fit, with its glazed expression and generally confused behaviour. This is the alternative explanation and it fits the recent finding that the 'rage syndrome' problem is reduced or removed by what the vets call 'a novel environment'. In other words, novelty and excitement cures the spaniel's acute boredom.

We spoke to one vet on this vexed issue and he confirmed that, in his opinion, 'rage syndrome' is a serious disease that requires detailed investigation with the full co-operation of all Cocker spaniel breeders. In his view all spaniels suffering from it should be put to sleep. We then spoke to Peggy Grayson, one of the top experts on gundogs, who has been judging spaniels at shows for over forty years. She bristled at the very mention of the term and boomed out her reply: 'The rage syndrome', she intoned, 'is the invention of trendy young vets, desperate for media coverage, suffering from verbal diarrhoea. That is all I have to say.' The Cocker spaniel she held in her arms showed no signs of disproving her. Such was her authority that it would never have dared.

The Return of the Flying Horse

The two young Brewster brothers from Lockerbie in the Scottish Borders might seem to have little in common with the medieval knights of Agincourt or Bannockburn, yet they share something very tangible – a love and respect for one of the most powerful animals ever to serve the human race.

Clydesdales are the gentle giants of the horse world. Their own breed standard stipulates they should have feet 'like a mason's mallet'. They stand proud, 17 hands tall at the withers, or shoulders, and up to 9 feet at the top of their head. A muscular stallion can weight up to a ton. Hardly the kind of pet or companion, you might think, for boys aged thirteen and eleven. Yet Tom and Ronald Brewster have no qualms. They call their own favourite gelding 'Disco', and describe him as 'big and cuddly'.

Despite his docile demeanour, Disco's ancestors were among the glory horses of history. In the Middle Ages ballad singers told of armoured knights on steeds that seemed to fly across the ground. The reality was far from our modern image of racing thoroughbreds. Horses that carried a knight in full armour had to be strong and sure-footed, endowed with enormous stamina and courage, utterly unflinching whatever they were asked to face. The great horses of Clydesdale were ideal for the battlefield and the joust. As early as the fifteenth century they were being exported to armies all over Europe. The precursors of the Duke of Hamilton's line, The Douglases of Clydesdale, played an important part in developing the trade.

As nations turned from warfare to develop their agriculture and trade, Flemish stallions were crossed with Scottish mares to provide horses with even more weight for pulling the plough. The Clydesdale, more or less as we know it today, became the muscle behind the growth in agriculture which fuelled the industrial revolution in the north of Britain. At their peak, in the nineteenth century, there were 140,000 of them in Scotland alone. As the British Empire spread, Clydesdales followed the emigrants to countries all over the world. In Australia they still recall the largest yoke ever assembled – seventy-six horses strung out in pairs to pull a 14-ton wagon of wool out of a flooded river.

It was the great stallions of the breed that helped to consolidate the Clydesdale's reputation. In the days before motorized transport, grooms led the best sires from farm to farm through the country lanes of Scotland and the northern counties so as to ensure that the finest bloodlines were maintained. Even today horse lovers argue about which was the best stallion of them all, but one name features prominently in most lists. Dunure Footprint is recorded to have fathered 146 foals in one year, his vigour maintained by feeding him the milk of two cows every day. Ironically it was in Dunure Footprint's own lifetime that the role of the Clydesdale passed its peak. He was born in

Tom and Ronald Brewster with their 1-ton pet Disco, a giant Clydesdale

75

The Brewster boys are joined by parents Tom and Cate

1908, and three years later the export of stallions reached a record level: over sixteen hundred of the best sailed for the United States and the Dominions. Before long the Clydesdales would be marshalled once again as war-horses, with huge, muscled shoulders hauling heavy guns and enormous loads of supplies through the clinging mud of Flanders and Northern France.

With the return of peace there came a new sound to the countryside, the motor tractor. As farming became more and more mechanized, field gates in Australia in the 1920s were thrown open and herds of Clydesdales were allowed to run free in the wild. The sight of a prime stallion and forty mares ranging the rough lands may have been impressive but their prospects of survival were small. Five centuries of partnership with mankind had ill-equipped them to forage for themselves. In Britain, too, their numbers diminished dramatically. Today there are only a hundred stallions and six hundred brood mares in the entire country.

Yet, far from lamenting its decline, Clydesdale admirers believe that the noble horse is now on its way back. Young Tom and Ronald are the fourth generation of Brewsters to share their lives with the breed. Their parents, Tom and Cate, have twenty-two of them on their Dumfries farm, including their own champion stallion, 'Bandirran Supreme', who responds more readily to his family name of 'Charlie'. Seeing Charlie leading his mares in a high-stepping charge over the young grass when the herd was liberated from its winter quarters left no doubt about the virility of the breed.

For the Brewsters the Clydesdales remain a rewarding business as well as part of the fabric of their family life. Their customers can expect to pay up to £4,000 for 'a real cracker'. Some buyers, like the big breweries, want them for show as images of a wholesome past. Others have found that the 1-ton horse can still deliver the goods when machines are breaking down. In the most severe of Canadian winters they still pull the feed out to cattle isolated by snow and ice. 'Disco', the eight-year-old gelding which carries the Brewster boys round the countryside on his broad back, is never likely to leave home, but there is a resurging demand from all over the world for his relatives. For Cate Brewster a departure is tinged with more than a little sadness.

'We live with them twenty-four hours a day and stay with a mare all night when she's foaling. I have to make a conscious effort not to love the horses too much. It breaks my heart to see them go'.

Today, when they do leave, they go in style. The Clydesdale no longer trudges to his new home or sails for weeks cooped up in the dark hold of a tramp steamer. The great beast now travels by air on scheduled cargo flights. That other flying horse, Pegasus, would have approved.

The Dog on the Silk Cushion

No other dog in the world has experienced a lifestyle like that of the royal Pekinese in the forty-eight palaces of old China. The attention that was paid to them is almost beyond belief. These revered palace Pekes feasted on shark fins, curlew liver and breast of quail. When thirsty they had a choice of antelope milk, tea brewed from spring buds, or soup made from sea swallows' nests. If, despite this gourmet fare, the little dogs fell sick, they were treated with an ointment of leopard's-leg fat and a throstle's eggshell full of custard-apple juice, in which had been dissolved three pinches of shredded rhino-horn. If this failed they were bled by the application of piebald leeches.

Theft of one of these small lap-dogs was punishable by death. So sacred were they that no one outside the royal palaces was allowed to set eyes upon them. Even the palace servants had to avert their eyes if they happened to encounter one of the Imperial dogs. The only exceptions to this rule were the four thousand eunuchs, whose special task was to tend to their every need and to supervise their breeding programmes. When new puppies arrived they were considered so precious that they were suckled not by the bitches, but by ladies-in-waiting.

If a special Peke took the ruler's fancy, it was instantly given high rank and possibly even created a duke or prince, with the appropriate royal revenues made available to ensure its comforts. The ritual of the canine toilet took hours to perform each day, bathing being followed by spraying with expensive perfumes. The dogs slept on exquisite, silken cushions.

Sarah meets Andrew Poon and his Peke

There was, however, a price to be paid for all this luxury. Drugs and mechanical devices were employed, with great cruelty, to stunt the growth of the young Pekes so that they would, as adults, be small enough to fit into the sleeves of the royal ladies. Some unfortunate pups were kept in tight wire corsets for days on end and allowed little or no exercise. Or they were held for hour after hour in the hands of eunuchs, gently squeezed and compressed in the hope that this would also prevent them from growing too large. Their noses were massaged to produce flatter faces. And all the time selective breeding was taking place to increase genetically these qualities of small body size and flat face.

Because of their restricted way of life, they were unknown in Britain even as late as the middle of the last century. The very first Pekinese dogs to arrive here were five animals looted from the Imperial Palace by British troops in 1860. When the soldiers stormed the palace its defenders killed all the royal dogs they could find, rather than let them fall into foreign hands. But in one room the intruders found five survivors next to the body of their protectress, a royal princess, who had committed suicide to avoid being captured. These animals were brought back as spoils of war and introduced the breed to Victorian England. Two were given to the Duchess of Richmond, two to the Duchess of Wellington, and the fifth was presented to Queen Victoria herself. This last animal, appropriately and unashamedly given the name of 'Looty', lived with the monarch as a much-loved pet for a further twelve years. It was commemorated in a portrait that still hangs at Buckingham Palace today.

These five animals served as the foundation stock for all our later Pekinese dogs and the breed quickly became one of the most popular lap-dogs in the country. In the decades that followed, many society ladies felt naked without their pet Pekes on their arms or in their laps. The appeal of these unusual dogs is clear enough. They are about the same weight and size as a human baby, have a flattened, infantile face, a rounded shape and clumsy locomotion resulting from their short, bent legs. Their fur is fluffy and soft to the touch. In other words, they possess all the qualities that make them into super-infants, ideal as child substitutes. But in personality they are anything but infantile, being stubborn, independent, dignified, loyal and courageous, to use the words mentioned by Peke owners in describing their dogs. They may look like infants to us, but they are still wolves at heart, like their ancient ancestors that roamed the forests thousands of years ago. It is, in fact, this wolf's brain inside a silky dwarf's body that gives the breed its special dignity. Nobody has been able to tell the Pekes that they have lost the wolf's fearsome jaws and great, muscular body, so they continue to behave as if they were still there. Hence their courage and their great spirit which appeals to all those who are not put off by their distorted canine form.

The Urban Goatherd

Rodgers and Hammerstein failed to get it quite right in *The Sound of Music*. Barbara Turnbull could have told them that no goatherd is ever lonely. Barbara is the urban goatherd of Carlisle, on the Scottish borders, and she has fourteen good reasons for leaving her bed at five o'clock in the morning. Standing literally at the bottom of her street, in a field in the middle of a large housing estate, is what is technically designated a herd of goats. But to Barbara each is an individual – one with a fondness for chewing cigarettes, another liable to go into a huff if

Sarah meets Barbara Turnbull and her herd of goats

spoken to in the wrong way, and all of them with a liking for a certain kind of mint with a hole.

The discovery that goats are individuals, rather than herd animals, was made early on, when Barbara acquired two of them with the idea of cutting down her household's large milk bills. Since then the numbers – and the rapport – have been growing. Each of the fourteen in her care has a name – Milly is the trouble-maker, Chloe is the aloof duchess, Katie is shy and needs attention, and Matilda rules the roost. For several of them, life with Barbara is a happy ending to a troubled past. Many had been ill-treated before they came into her care, and the larger her collection has grown, the further her reputation has spread. Now any stray or needy goat in the district is liable to end up in her refuge. Some have suffered because of the mistaken notion that goats are hardy, needing little attention or dietary care. In truth they need shelter from wind and rain, for there is little insulating fat beneath the skin and the fleece lacks the water-repellent property of the sheep's. Goats are also choosy about the food they eat, and need to have their intake from grazing supplemented.

Yet the rewards from this remarkable relationship are not all one-sided. By half past five in the morning, Barbara will be hard at work milking her herd, supplying not only her own fridge but also that of anyone in the area who cannot tolerate cow's milk. To the little lad with a delicate skin condition and the pensioner on a strict diet, Barbara's herd has become a vital part of their well-being.

The most fascinating aspect of Barbara's relationship with her goats is their growing closeness. At one time this would not have seemed at all remarkable, for in earlier times goats lived with and not just alongside us. Indeed they were accepted as companions of the hearth. Only convention and a basic lack of space prevent Barbara from doing likewise. She would happily have them in her home as household pets. If she is tired or depressed, they seem to have an intuitive understanding. They gather round and nuzzle close, sensing her need for the warm companionship they can offer. If

she feels angry or tetchy, they will frisk with her gently until her natural good humour is restored.

Life with the goats is full of the unexpected, especially as seven of them are still kids. Watching them bound and gambol in the field has shown Barbara how much they respond to freedom, rather than being tethered to a peg. In the wild they would not only scale mountain slopes, they would also happily clamber up a convenient tree. Barbara's fondest memory of the kids is the night all seven squeezed through the fence bordering their field and followed her quietly home in a neat, orderly line. It took all her strength to get them to return.

It has not always been easy to keep the goats well fed, warmly sheltered and with sufficient space to live happily. But Barbara Turnbull, like her goats, is an intrepid and enterprising spirit. Little is allowed to stand in her way. If you tell her she is a stubborn old goat, she will simply thank you for the compliment.

The Dog that became an Ornament

Generally accepted as the smallest breed of dog in the world, the minute Chihuahua was once known as the Ornament dog. Its amazingly small size enabled it to be worn on the body like an unusual piece of jewelry, or tucked into a fold of clothing as if it were a living corsage.

Despite being a dwarf among dogs, however, the Chihuahua retains all the canine qualities of the large breeds. It is an intelligent, lively animal that still requires a great deal of exercise and does not take kindly to being treated constantly as a decorative toy.

Hilary Harmar, a world authority on Chihuahuas, believes that the breed originated in Mexico. She discovered a remote Indian village in the Chihuahua district where 'nearly all the Indians keep easily recognizable Chihuahuas, all with the curious bark, the typical long foot, the molera and the large round eyes, and flat tail so distinctive of the breed.' She points out that there seems no conceivable reason for the Indians keeping this breed unless it has long had a role in their society. And she adds that it is significant that the ancient Aztecs had a saying: 'If you drink water, do not make a noise sucking it in: you are not a little dog.' One of the unique features of the Chihuahua is that it drinks water in a highly distinctive and conspicuously noisy manner. So it would seem that this little dog really has been in Mexico for many centuries, long before the arrival of the Europeans.

She sees the special role of these dogs in early American Indian society as having been personal pets kept for sacrificial use. At the death of the dog's owner, the unfortunate animal would be killed and cremated with the human body. This was done to provide the spirit of the dead person with a guide to see him safely across the nine rivers of the fearful underworld.

Eileen Goodchild, another expert, disagrees strongly with this view of the Chihuahua's beginnings. She believes that it was the Europeans who took the animal to Mexico *after* the Spanish conquest in the sixteenth century. She traces its origins back to early Egypt, where mummified remains of the breed are said to have been found, dating back to 1000 B.C. From there it spread along the North African coast to Carthage and was carried to the island of Malta by the Carthaginians around 100 B.C. On the small island of Malta it thrived and was given the local name of Kelb Ta But, or Pocket dog. From Malta it was carried to mainland Europe where it was portrayed in a painting that predates the voyage of Columbus to the Americas by ten years. The painting in question is a Sistine Chapel fresco by Botticelli called 'The Sons of Moses', painted in 1482 and showing a boy carrying a tiny dog that is almost identical with the modern Chihuahua.

Supporting this 'European' view is the fact that the Chihuahua is still a popular dog in Malta today and appears to have been the true 'Maltese' dog of earlier times. The dog we call the Maltese today is not known on the island,

Mexico or Egypt? Did the Chihuahua travel from west to east or vice versa?

suggesting that at some stage there has been a confusion of identity between the two breeds. There are therefore two opposing views that are irreconcilable and we must await further evidence to decide finally whether the tiny dog travelled East to West or West to East across the Atlantic Ocean some centuries ago.

Coming to more recent times the picture is much clearer. We talked to Dick Dickinson who is the Chairman of the Chihuahua Club of America about the arrival of the midget breed on the show dog scene. He explained that it was during the Mexican honeymoon of his grandparents that they encountered this animal and were so enchanted by it that they brought several specimens back to the United States with them when their holiday was over. That was in 1897 and some years later they founded the Chihuahua Club of America, watching their chosen breed become increasingly popular as the years passed. In 1904 only five were registered in the USA. In 1958 there were over forty-eight thousand registrations. The Chihuahua was here to stay.

From the United States the breed has spread all over the world and is now popular in almost every country where dog shows are held. Its height is between 6 and 8 inches and its weight no more than 2 to 6 pounds. The smallest dogs are the ones most strongly favoured and ideally the weight should not exceed 4 pounds – a mere pocketful of dog. In temperament it is described as 'active and bold', and it makes an ideal companion for anyone with limited living space. If it has a drawback it is that small children are liable to treat it as a wind-up toy and handle it too harshly.

The Smartest Cat of All

Even among those who opt for other breeds, the Siamese is generally considered to be the smartest cat of all. It is certainly one of the most popular. Yet just a century ago, when it was first shown at the Crystal Palace in London, the Siamese was viewed with marked suspicion. One critic of the time dismissed it as 'a nightmare of a cat'. What he was seeing of course was a cat quite unlike any which had been brought to Britain before.

Although the origin of the Siamese is lost in antiquity, some experts believe that it must have developed over the ages from the highly-prized temple cat of Burma. Others trace its development back even further to the sacred cat of ancient Egypt, a theory that finds support in its close resemblance to sculptures of the cat goddess, Bast. Whichever of the theories is correct, there is no doubt that the cat flourished in Siam for at least two hundred years before the Victorians finally managed to introduce it to Britain.

In Siam itself the ownership of this beautiful

The distinctive Siamese cat

cat was strictly limited to members of the royal family. Only the most distinguished emissaries were allowed to have some, as gifts. Indeed it is on record that it took several years of careful diplomatic negotiation with the King of Siam before Britain's General Walker got permission for his daughter to take the first male and two females to Britain.

At best, the Siamese is a svelte, medium-sized and beautifully balanced animal which moves with the considered grace of a jungle creature. Whatever their eventual markings, all kittens will be born pure white. The colouring, known as the points, develops later and always appears at the colder extremities of the body such as the ears, the mask, the tail and the paws. The coat colour in the original sealpoint variety is cream, shading to a light warm fawn on the back where it is connected to the dark ears by a light but well-defined tracing. In the best show specimens the light body colour and the uniformly dark points will contrast strongly. Occasionally, though, an owner will get a surprise. If a cat has a bad leg and it is bandaged, the points can lose their colour. Happily this is usually only temporary.

Apart from its appearance, the temperament of the Siamese explains its growth in popularity over the past hundred years. Most of the early ones brought into Britain had squints and kinked tails, characteristics once regarded as desirable but now recognised in the show world as serious faults. Legend has it that the kinks came from the princesses in the royal palace in Siam hanging their rings on the cats' tails.

The Siamese is a very playful cat which can be warmly affectionate when it chooses and haughtily independent when it feels otherwise. Give it plenty of toys and it will make a bright and highly intelligent pet. Most of all give it your own companionship or, if you have to be out all day, that of another Siamese. It frets if it is left alone and responds most positively to the company of people. When we visited the Scottish cat show in Glasgow, some owners assured us that their Siamese could even understand what was being said to them.

That, it must be acknowledged, requires a very smart cat indeed.

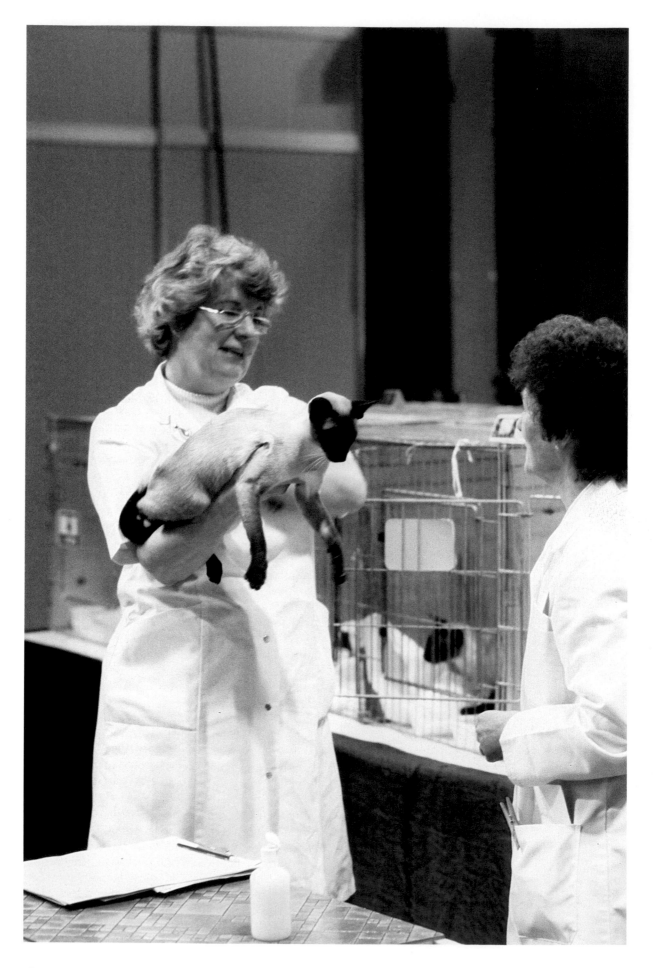

The Dog with Matchstick Legs

So frail does the little Italian greyhound look that one author, writing about the breed some time ago, gave serious instructions on how to pick the diminutive animal up without breaking it. In reality it is much tougher than it looks and one owner observed his Italian greyhound leaping 15 feet down from an open window and then, after a brief shake, running off across a lawn, all its four matchstick legs perfectly intact.

It is perhaps the look of frailty, however, that has worked against the popularity of this breed and kept its numbers down. In the last edition of its Stud Book the Kennel Club records only

The Italian greyhound – an aristocrat which can sprint at 40 m.p.h.

ninety registrations for the year, which puts it almost into the category of a rare breed. In a recent survey in the United States, it only managed to come eighty-second in the top hundred breeds.

Examining it closely, its legs do seem to be so very long and so very slender, that to have such a dog running around your feet as you move about the house must be a constant concern. One false step could cause serious damage. And the little creature looks so terribly emaciated at the same time, as though it is starving even when it has been plied with the choicest titbits. But appearances are deceptive and the enthusiastic owners of Italian greyhounds are happy to defend their chosen breed against all such criticisms. All they will admit to as a problem is that the slender shape of the animal's body and its short coat do mean that it cannot stand very cold weather and hates high winds. But that apart it apparently makes an ideal pet, with a delightful if slightly reserved temperament.

It is certainly a dog with a long history and, judging by early paintings, it has changed remarkably little over the centuries, unlike so many other show breeds that have been continually modified and exaggerated. It may be a miniature breed, but it does not suffer from any of the usual problems of 'dwarfism', such as the alteration of its basic proportions. It retains the same beauty and grace as a full-sized greyhound, and if you have no way of telling its size in a photograph, it is hard to guess just how small it really is.

The ancient Egyptians had already developed a slender greyhound type of dog, as we know from their tomb paintings, and in all probability they had also started to miniaturize this type of dog by selective breeding to create a high-status court dog to adorn the cushions and floors of palace rooms. From there the little dogs no doubt made their way to Rome and became established as the play-things of the nobility, spreading out eventually to all the courts of Europe as the centuries passed. The fifteenth-century artists Jan van Eyck and Hans Memling both included Italian greyhounds in their paintings. In Britain it became a fashionable breed in the Tudor and Stuart

periods, and by the start of the nineteenth century its popularity had become so great that it was vying with the little Maltese and the King Charles spaniel for the role of the top toy dog in high society.

Royalty have frequently fallen under its spell and monarchs who have owned Italian greyhounds include Charles I, Queen Anne, Queen Victoria and Frederick the Great, not to mention the African King Lobengula who fell in love with one to such an extent that he exchanged two hundred head of Matabele cattle in order to possess it.

Sadly, by the middle of the last century, the craze for producing smaller and smaller specimens was resulting in unsound animals and as a result the breed nearly became extinct. But then in 1890 serious breeders took over from the commercial dog dealers in handling the breed and saved it for posterity, returning it to its former, stronger self. Today it is as hardy as it has ever been, thanks to the work of dedicated enthusiasts.

We spoke to a breed specialist, Anna Marshall, and asked her whether, in her opinion, the slender creature she was holding could compete in a race against its larger relatives. She felt that, over very short sprints, it could give them a good run for their money, but not over longer races. It can reach speeds of 40 miles an hour in short spurts, but cannot maintain this for very long. All the same, it is quite capable of catching hares on the run and loves flushing birds from cover. But there is no doubt that it is in its element as a pampered pet, reclining elegantly on a velvet cushion, slender legs dangling gracefully over the edge. It has been bred for so long for this lifestyle that it has now become one of the true aristocrats of the dog world.

The Cat who's not so Dim

Those who call the long-haired cat the dimmest of all cats will get no support from Grace Pond, who is an international expert on the breed. Dim cats, she replies firmly, usually have dim owners. The Longhairs may be quieter than other types of cat but they do have a lot of personality and respond to human attention with affection.

The cat with the face that launched a thousand chocolate boxes has certainly been popular in Europe for well over four hundred years, even if its origins are shrouded in mystery. Early authorities suggested that its parentage might have included the full-coated wild cat or possibly the Pallas cat, named after the explorer who first saw it in Asia. Both possibilities have since been discounted. The first record of the long-haired cat in Europe in fact dates back to the middle of the sixteenth century when they were introduced to Italy by the traveller Pietro Della Valle. The seventeenth-century naturalist Buffon described them as Angoras after the city (now called Ankara) where they were believed to originate.

The long fur probably evolved in the first place through a spontaneous mutation in mountainous areas such as Turkey and Persia. This theory was certainly reinforced when a fresh strain of Turkish cat was brought to Britain just over thirty years ago. They had been

discovered in the area around Lake Van, which had been inaccessible until fairly recently. The cats were similar in appearance to the original Angoras and were found to breed true: kittens born to them were always like their parents in appearance.

The original Angoras had small heads, tallish ears and rangy bodies, and their fur was long rather than luxurious. As their popularity spread they were crossed with other long-coated cats reputed to come from Persia, which had rounder heads, sturdier bodies and fluffier tails. The strong features of the Persian predominated. Gradually the Angora seemed

to disappear and all long-haired cats were described as Persians. It is the name by which they are still known in North America and other parts of the world, although the governing council of the Cat Fancy in Britain prefers to embrace historical accuracy by calling them simply Longhairs.

Whatever their genetic origin, no one can deny the enormous appeal that long-haired cats have for human beings. They are in effect a symbol of quiet and placid opulence, coveted as pets by devotees ranging from Queen Victoria to the enemies of James Bond. Their attraction is undoubtedly a mixture of temperament and appearance. Ian Fleming's characters may have opted for the white: they could equally have chosen the Blue, the Chinchilla, the Tortoiseshell, the Pewter, the Chocolate or the Lilac.

It was a black long-haired kitten which sparked off Grace Pond's devotion to the breed when she was presented with one as a gift at the age of four. The young animal brought her childhood to life and Longhairs have been part of her family ever since. During the Second World War her son's small cat was buried in the ruins when their home was blitzed. The family lost everything and moved to the country to live with her mother. Three weeks later they were astonished to learn that, incredibly, the cat had managed to struggle out of the debris and set out to find them.

It is devotion of that kind which makes the long-haired cat so appealing to so many people, although Grace would be the first to emphasize that the relationship brings its demands as well as its rewards. The coat of a Longhair can look quite spectacular, particularly with its attractive ruff framing its vivid eyes, but the only way to keep it beautiful is by daily grooming of up to twenty minutes. When Grace once got carried away and let her stock grow to sixteen cats, she quickly learned that her days were no longer her own. Longhairs certainly know how to pose and are not as dim as some people believe.

The Dog that moves like a Goldfish

When the Peking Kennel Club first recorded a breed standard for the Shih Tzu it demanded that this little dog should display 'lion head, bear torso, camel hoof, feather-duster tail, palm-leaf ears, rice teeth, pearly petal tongue and movement like a goldfish'. This is asking a lot, but it is easy to see how the Shih Tzu inspired such a poetic description. Its dominant feature, its extremely long hair, hangs right down to the ground so that when it walks rapidly forward the animal appears to be gliding along like a fish swimming smoothly through water.

In addition to its remarkable physical appearance, the Shih Tzu is also a breed of strong character. It has been developed over centuries as a pampered palace favourite in its oriental homelands. Precisely which palace was involved in the first instance, however,

The appealing Shih Tzu

remains a disputed question. One school of thought sees the Shih Tzu as a Tibetan breed, developed as the Tibetan Lion dog in the Lhasa palace of the Dalai Lama and sent by him as tribute to the Chinese rulers in Peking. There it is supposed to have been modified to suit the local tastes, selective breeding having been applied to produce a dog with a rounder skull, flatter face, wider chest and shorter legs. Some believe that this was achieved by the simple measure of crossing the Tibetan dogs (of Lhasa Apso type) with local Pekinese dogs, and it has to be admitted that today's Shih Tzus do look remarkably like intermediates between Apsos and Pekes.

A second school of thought prefers to look upon the Shih Tzu as a palace breed developed in China alongside the Pekinese. It points out that there are references in an early travel book to a long-haired dog in Peking and mention of 'a pair of beautiful Chinese dogs' in the menagerie of the Dalai Lama, implying that the Shih Tzus were taken from Peking to Lhasa, rather than the other way around.

The truth is that there was probably a great deal of back-and-forth movement between the two palaces over the centuries, as the balance of power shifted between China and Tibet. With each change, these small palace dogs, being symbols of high status and nobility, would have been an inevitable part of tributes, spoils, appeasement gestures, and goodwill gifts. (This oriental habit persists to this day, but with Giant Pandas taking the role of 'prestige gifts' in place of the little Lion dogs.) With each shift in power, new breeding possibilities were opened up to those in charge of the palace menageries and new modifications to the size, shape and colour of the sacred palace dogs could be attempted. We may never be able to unravel the whole story or pin-point the very first development of the various noble breeds, but we can be certain that, until the early part of the twentieth century, dogs such as the Shih Tzu and the Lhasa Apso were not for the eyes of the ordinary people. Now, in the last half-century, all this has changed and both

Ann Wynyard, a leading expert on oriental breeds, with a champion Shih Tzu

these breeds have become increasingly popular around the globe as attractive, small companion dogs for huge numbers of enthusiasts.

We asked Ann Wynyard, author of *Dogs of Tibet* and an expert on oriental breeds, to explain the appeal of the Shih Tzu to modern dog owners. In her view the fact that the breed has enjoyed centuries of devoted care and attention from the palace eunuchs in the Far East has ensured that it has developed a unique personality and a high level of intelligence. 'The Shih Tzu breed is capable of giving utter devotion and hours of fun and amusement – but he is still an aristocrat and considers that he is your equal and not your servant – and is even possibly your superior!' She also makes the point that, with his palace background, the Shih Tzu does not take kindly to being left alone: 'If he does not get plenty of human companionship he is unable to develop his full character. His character is very versatile – so what more could you want of any breed?'

In answer to this last question, perhaps one could have asked for a more attractive name. Many people find that pronouncing the Chinese title 'Shih Tzu' sounds at best impolite and at worst like a curse. Those who have been worrying about this problem might be interested to know that the officially recommended rendering 'shid-zoo' is in fact an error. The correct Chinese pronunciation is apparently more like 'sher-zer'. This may be more polite but it still lacks appeal. Perhaps the time has come to find a purely English name that is appealing enough to match its owner.

Oscar and the Owlman

With his huge eyes and hooked beak, Oscar the owl is a formidable sight even when he is perched sedately on the arm of seventeen-year-old Jonathan Hodges. A European Eagle owl, weighing all of 5½ pounds, can be rather fierce when provoked. But, in the eyes of Oscar, Jonathan is no ordinary human being. The teenager puts it modestly: 'He thinks I'm his dad.'

In fact, Jonathan's achievement is already remarkable. He has one of the largest private collections of birds of prey in Britain. His interest in them was kindled just five years ago by his first visit to a falconry display. Shortly

Oscar and Jonathan Hodges

afterwards he discovered his natural ability to rear chicks to become fully-grown adult birds. Walking round his home in the countryside near Stoke in Staffordshire, you will hear him being greeted by his 'family'. They include Ollie, another Eagle owl, Tchuke the Snowy owl, Rocky the Barn owl and two Tawny owls called Snip and Snap.

All of them were hand-reared from the nest and now regard Jonathan as a kind of surrogate parent, calling whenever he comes near. In the evening he takes them inside the house, in turn, to spend time sitting on his arm tethered to a glove, getting accustomed to being with him in all sorts of circumstances. With infinite patience, he trains them to fly to him by a reward system of feeding them titbits.

Behind all of this lies Jonathan's growing concern for the diminishing number of owls in the British countryside. Many have been the victims of pesticides and others are finding that their old nesting sites of farmyard barns are being replaced by unsuitable corrugated sheds. Jonathan would like more farmers to put up nesting boxes. Although his imprinted birds

At seventeen, Jonathan is campaigning for the owls of the British countryside

would never survive in the wild, he is preparing to breed chicks which can fly free to repopulate the countryside.

It may have started as a hobby but for Jonathan it is already becoming a way of life. After trying a youth training scheme when he left school a year ago, he soon returned to his birds, writing to some forty schools in the Staffordshire area, offering to bring his birds and give illustrated talks to children to make them more aware of nature. It has been so successful that he and his parents are planning a specialist holiday for bird lovers in the Churnet valley where they now live.

One of Jonathan's greatest pleasures is to share his environment with the owls, on their own terms. Out in the dark, flying Oscar to a lure, he knows that the bird can see him even when he can see nothing: 'He trusts me and I trust him: that's all there is to it.'

The Bulldog Breed

Strolling down the King's Road in Chelsea with Cuthbert the Bulldog can be quite an experience. His owner, David McHale, is uncanny at predicting how strangers will react. Pretty models say Cuthbert is lovely and want to cuddle him. Big fat people tend to grimace and say what an ugly dog. Cuthbert, of course, is aloof from all of this. He is a champion of the Bulldog breed, the dog whose nature has become a symbol of the British character.

Not that it was always like this. In darker and more violent times, the ancestors of Cuthbert were deliberately bred for fighting bulls. In fact, the flesh of the bull baited in this way was believed to be more succulent. Bull-fighting dogs were short of leg and strong of jaw, designed to crawl along the ground on their bellies and then hold on to the poor bull until it succumbed. These dogs were often subjected to harrowing treatment to make them better fighters. Lower lips were amputated and facial features reshaped with blocks and clamps, all in the interest of allowing the dog to breathe more easily while maintaining a grim hold on the bull.

Even the abolition of the barbaric sport in 1835 brought little relief for the Bulldog. When the Humane Act made baiting illegal, Bulldog owners simply allowed the dogs to fight each

David McHale introduces two of his Bulldogs

other, and the sporting public of the time eagerly followed their careers, as we do famous human fighters of today. It is easy for us to think that the dogs were forced to do battle. In truth their background and training made them eager to fight, often to the death. Stringent conditions were laid down to ensure fair play – including a bizarre rule for 'tasting the dog', which required a neutral steward to lick the combatants' coats to ensure that no destructive dressings had been applied.

Ironically it was the dogfight itself which brought relief for the unfortunate British breed. The Bulldog's short legs were not made for the sharp, speedy movements which often

93

decided a contest. Attention turned to other, more nimble breeds. The Bulldog became an anachronism, known for the lexicon of expressions it had given to the English language. 'Coming up to scratch' originally denoted the white line where dogs faced each other in the pit. 'Top dog' and 'bottom dog' described positions in the fight.

Yet the legacy of the Bulldog was more than that. For courage and tenacity it became legendary, and the Victorians took it to their hearts as a symbol of defiant determination. The Bulldog Club, founded in 1875, proudly claims to be the first specialist club for any breed of dog. Cartoonists in such magazines as *Punch* saw in it the very essence of Britishness – John Bull anthropomorphically carried the flag.

At the same time, human expectations of the Bulldog were changing. The ferocious animal of the bullring was seen in a very different light in the burgeoning world of the dog show, where the breeding standard for bulldogs required the animals to be 'humorous'. Bulldogs were expected to exhibit a sour but intelligent expression and a proud stance, but their whole way of going about things was to be funny.

Cuthbert, or to give him his proud and proper name Jacob of Belloc, certainly possesses the personality that any judge would look for in one of the most successful show champions of recent years. Yet Bulldogs are far from being creatures of comic derision, and David McHale understands well why the breed is so identified with the character of the British people. Bulldogs are easy-going, he says, until they are upset – and that only happens when they are pushed very hard. Neither emotional nor excitable, and rarely aggressive, they are in fact the complete opposite of how they look.

Perhaps that explains why Cuthbert is so much in demand for promotions and advertising, and causes a minor sensation wherever he goes. Wearing his Union Jack waistcoat, Cuthbert loves to bait not a bull but a ball. Show him a football and you will only get away when, inevitably, his strong teeth coupled with his enthusiasm prove too great and it bursts. Even then he will hang on for grim life to the tattered remains. Like Winston Churchill, Cuthbert never gives up.

When Love laughed at Locksmiths

No one who has seen the new breed of Burmilla cat can doubt its attraction. With its glowing coat and gentle nature it is instantly appealing both as a household pet and as an animal for showing. Its expressive eyes range in colour from warm chartreuse to an emerald green and are rimmed with the kind of black eye lining that a beautician would take ages to achieve. No wonder their admirers sport car stickers announcing: 'I love the Burmilla'.

Yet the Burmilla is an accident. Even the Baroness Miranda von Kirchberg, who was instrumental in bringing the breed into being, would not deny Nature the final credit. The Burmilla appeared, in her own words, 'when love laughed at locksmiths'.

The Baroness is a patron of the Cat Survival Trust and of the Exotic Pets Refuge. For many years she has been an eminent breeder of one of the most aristocratic of all cats, the Russian Blue. In 1982 her peers voted her 'the most outstanding breeder of the year'. Not one to be attracted by genetic tinkering, Miranda is a perfectionist; there is no place in her world for the eccentric and the accidental.

So it was until Fabergé met Sanquist. Although their breeds are totally different, the two were drawn to each other from the start. However much they were kept apart, they seemed to want to play together. Fabergé, of course, is a queen: fanciers use the name for breeding females. With her short, sleek coat and golden eyes, she is of the exotic Burmese breed which was first brought to Britain in 1949. Sanquist is very different, a long-haired Chinchilla with a silver coat to complement his

Baroness Miranda and the Burmilla

emerald eyes. Male cats, even the finest, are simply called studs.

Pedigree matings were planned for each of them with cats of their own type. When Fabergé came into season, she was carefully locked away to await her honeymoon. No one knows how it happened but the door to her room must have been opened. When Fabergé's four kittens duly arrived, they were short-haired and attractive but clearly not Burmese. They had the sparkling silver coat of Sanquist, their father. The Burmilla was born.

Accidents have been known to happen occasionally in the world of pedigree cats. Generally the kittens are neutered and live happy lives as domestic pets. But Miranda quickly realized that these kittens were very special. Apart from an enchanting temperament, they had a remarkable health record. They had none of the kitten ailments which can be expected, not even sticky eyes: 'They were the fattest, healthiest, perkiest kittens I had ever known.' They were also much more like their Burmese mother than their Chinchilla father. Normally one could expect the kittens to be about 50 per cent of each parent, but these were a surprisingly good Burmese type enhanced by the silver colouring of the Chinchilla.

The Baroness decided to try to establish them as a new breed, a major undertaking in the cat world which has strict regulations for proving and maintaining the characteristics of different types of cat. In order to be granted recognition a variety has to prove three generations of pure breeding. It also has to show that a reasonable number of the variety is being bred and that a sufficient number or breeders is interested in producing them.

The first step seemed almost insurmountable. The four kittens were all female, with the delightful names of Galatea, Gemma, Gabriella and Gisella. When Galatea and Gemma were subsequently mated, the stud in each case was a Burmese. The Burmilla characteristics were maintained. The family tree had begun to grow. Miranda von Kirchberg helped to draft the preliminary standard of points for judging the Burmilla. She also formed the Burmilla Association which agreed a careful breeding policy. Another distinguished breeder, Therese Clarke, bought Gemma to

establish her own line, and she has since launched the Burmilla Cat Club.

Officially the Burmilla is still an 'experimental silver of Burmese type'. Already there are more than a hundred of them in Britain and others have been exported to the United States, France and Denmark. The number of breeders is now well into double figures. The Cat Association has given the Burmilla 'provisional' acceptance. In time, admirers hope the Cat Fancy will follow. As the fourth generation begins to appear, Burmilla owners are carefully meeting the stipulations which will lead to full, official recognition.

A Dog of Distinction

The Poodle has been much maligned. Mention the name and for most people 'French', 'frivolous' and occasionally 'freaky' will spring to mind. Such a reputation is quite unfair to an animal with antecedents in several European countries, which was once a hard-working gundog, during which service its bizarre top-knot hairdo evolved.

To trace in any detail the far-flung lineage of such a dog is difficult, but somewhere along the way the Poodle must have been set apart as a distinct breed. Known in Russia as *Pudel*, in France as *Berbet*, and in Germany as *Pudeln* ('to splash around in water'), centuries ago it retrieved ducks from the muddy lakes and ponds of Europe. To facilitate swimming, its hindquarters were shaved; later, clusters or 'bobbles' of hair were left to protect the joints from rheumatism. Hair was tied back from the eyes, first with string, then with coloured ribbon to assist identification. But the Poodle

The flamboyant style of clip which reflects the social history of the Poodle

It has been gundog, war dog, circus performer – and devoted friend

was still hundreds of years away from the Boulevards of the Left Bank and the front cover of *Vogue*.

Few will recall the Poodle's history as an active soldier. In the Napoleonic wars, they were employed carrying bandages to the wounded. At Austerlitz, 'Moustache' (the most famous of his number) rescued the fallen Regimental colours and carried them to his colonel, despite having a badly wounded paw. For this deed he was decorated for valour. Much later in

the nineteenth century, the Poodle earned his keep as a circus performer with generations of French clowns.

Perhaps the present-day prima donna of the show-ring, requiring hours of grooming and attention, owes its status to Louis XVI, in whose reign the art of clipping was completely divorced from the trimming necessary for duck-hunting, and the unfortunate dogs found themselves decorated with lover's knots, coats of arms and grotesque pompadours like those worn by their mistresses at court.

No longer a water retriever and wearing styles somewhat subdued and standardized, the modern Poodle is a triumph of human frivolity. But although it would not be too far-fetched to suppose that a certain amount of wig powder at the court of Versailles found its way into the coiffure of the Poodles, lacquer (the modern equivalent) is discouraged, as is hair dyeing. Many nationalities still parade their eccentricities on the backs of the Poodle, however – a sort of canine topiary reflecting the vicissitudes of social history. Today's clips include the English Saddle and the Royal Dutch. Unlike Samson, though, the cutting of hair has not robbed the Poodle of its essential strengths, and in the transition to show dog it has managed to keep its earlier breed character.

The Light of Freedom

Redundancy has become a liberating word for the pit ponies which laboured in the coal mines of Britain for well over three hundred years. Early in this century, there were more than seventy-one thousand ponies labouring underground in an environment unnatural to both beast and man. Today only forty remain, all in pits with a short life expectancy: they too will soon be walking into the light of day.

Behind the pit ponies lies one of the most remarkable stories of a partnership between animal and man. It was in the early part of the seventeenth century, with improved pumping and ventilation, that it became possible for horses to survive underground. Before then they had worked on the surface hauling coal for

Even in retirement Tom Crossan maintains his affinity with the pit ponies he first met underground

as long as mines had existed. As they went down the pits, they took over the heavy work previously done by women and often children.

From the very beginning the type of horse used was determined by the height of the seam. The diminutive Shetland was always popular; so too was the sturdy Welsh mountain pony. The demands of the work would exact a fearsome toll. Ponies as well as people could fall victim all to easily to the coal dust disease silicosis. Yet, in this unlikely environment, the bonds that grew between pony and miner often were very close. In many pit disasters the ponies were given precedence over the men, who waited until they had been led to safety first. In the Stanley pit disaster of 1909 a young miner who went back to rescue his stranded animal was later rewarded with the pony as a token of his bravery.

Tom Crossan was a lad of barely fourteen when he had to give up his hopes of working in a stable and went down the Durham pits instead. He found the ponies waiting for him, and a friendship was started which has grown throughout his working life. Not that it began auspiciously: in his first year one flighty pony

99

kicked out his two front teeth and left him concussed for three days. For all that, Tom's affection for his mining companions is total. He still talks of one 'little devil' barely 8 hands high who brought a lot of laughter to the coal face. In those days, the colliers kept their water in tin bottles which they left hanging on a hook. When no one was looking, the little pony would bite out the cork and tip the bottle for a refreshing drink. 'The only way you knew he had been there was when you found the neck squashed by his teeth.'

It was in 1909 that the first campaign was launched to bring the pit ponies out of the dark. When Francis A. Cox founded the National Equine Defence League, he had vocal support from the Home Secretary, Winston Churchill, and such writers as John Galsworthy and Jerome K. Jerome. Some early achievements were to limit the weight the ponies hauled and to define their working day as the same as the

men's, eight hours on and sixteen hours off.

Since then the League has worked to improve their conditions and to provide a retirement home for them when eventually they can walk into the light. Visiting the League's sanctuary at Oak Tree Farm, just outside Carlisle, you can see the ponies in the fields sniffing the spring air with a special relish. When they first arrive, they often have to be kept for a time in enclosed stalls until they adjust. After a working life on dried food, they need to be weaned on to a natural diet. Outside the fields are lush and green and waiting.

The sanctuary's director, Frank Tebbitt, speaks of the joy of seeing them eventually running in the fields or lying on their backs kicking their legs in the air. 'It's back to nature as far as they are concerned, and they love it.' Happily some of the sanctuary's ponies have been there for twenty years, even longer than they spent out of the light.

Cinderella is still at the Ball

Nineteenth-century mill workers from Yorkshire would scarely recognize today the scruffy terrier which used to hunt for vermin among the bales of raw wool in the dark factories of the north. Like Cinderella, it has been transformed into a thing of real beauty – and the ball is still in progress.

In many ways the story of the Yorkshire terrier is one of the most remarkable in the world of dogs, for they were brought into being, literally, by the industrial revolution. Among the flying shuttles and clanking looms of the mill towns, nature worked her own genetic chemistry with a conglomeration of indeterminate breeds to produce one of the loveliest dogs of today. In just over a century, the ratters from the woollen mills have become the cosseted companions of the rich and the famous, and the pride of more than fourteen thousand admirers in Britain alone. The lists of the Kennel Club show they are the most popular toy dog in existence.

The toy dog produced by the industrial revolution

Where did they come from? And how did they develop? Even the fathers of the Kennel Club could provide no certain credentials when they first tried to categorize the breed in the stud book of 1874. By calling it 'a broken-haired Scotch terrier or Yorkshire terrier', they indicated that its metamorphosis was not complete even then. It was several years later, after loving improvement in Yorkshire, that its present name was confirmed.

Although no firm record exists, the history of the breed can be traced back to the early 1800s when many Scots were attracted to Yorkshire by the mills of the rapidly advancing industrial revolution. As trade flourished in the aftermath of the Napoleonic Wars, there were jobs for entire families – husbands, wives and often young children – as well as their dogs.

Bales of unprocessed wool in the primitive factories were a warren for vermin, and the Scots brought with them an assorted army of ferocious hunters – the broken-haired Scotch terrier, the Paisley, the Clydesdale, the Waterside and the distinctive Skye terrier. These dogs were fierce in their devotion to individual humans who lavished on them the affection that needed a focus in such a bleak environment.

No one can doubt that the dog which emerged from this melting-pot is, at its best, one of nature's works of art. Its breed standard is the only one (out of more than 150) that demands metallic colours. The tan on the heads and legs should gleam like a golden sovereign. The body coat should be the blue of dark steel, shining like a polished gun barrel reflecting the sun on a summer's day. What makes the breed truly exceptional is the length and quality of the hair. Fully groomed, with a parting from nose to tail, it can hang all the way from the back to the ground. The hair itself has a texture similar to human hair, and each individual strand feels like silk.

Many people attribute the Yorkie's remarkable hair to early attempts at improving the breed by crossing it with the Maltese terrier and the English toy terrier. Yorkshire folklore has a different explanation, which recently acquired some scientific validity. When the earliest terriers hunted vermin in the mills they became coated in the grease used to protect the woollen bales. The mill workers organized contests to find the terrier with the longest hair and noticed that the grease deposit appeared to improve the coats. Eventually, when it was refined, the grease was found to contain a high proportion of lanolin, a basic ingredient of many of today's human shampoos.

Whatever the explanation for their coats, modern Yorkies need a lot of devoted attention if they are to look their best. The preparation rings at a dog show are like hairdressing salons, with the dogs draped, in the style of *Coronation Street*, with paper rollers. The practical purpose is to ensure that the hair ends will not split and that the coat will emerge in all its soft, metallic glory. In the words of a leading judge, Les Griffiths, preparing a dog for showing is 'like nurturing an orchid in a greenhouse'. Brushed out and with its hair ribboned in a perky top knot, it is a sight few people can resist. But, lest you think the Yorkie has become little more than an ornament, its terrier characteristics remain. It is lovable and devoted to its owners and assertive and guarded

Les Griffiths with Yorkies awaiting the show-ring

with strangers. Bigger dogs usually back off when a Yorkie gives them a warning.

In many ways this mixture of character and beauty is what has made the breed such a universal pet. When Les Griffiths left the Royal Air Force forty years ago he wanted to buy a gift for his wife Hilda, who disliked dogs. He bought her a Yorkshire terrier. 'They're not dogs to us,' says Les. 'They're family.' From their home near Pontefract in West Yorkshire, he and Hilda have travelled the world judging Yorkshire terriers. At the last count Les had been to Tokyo six times.

Elizabeth Taylor would understand their devotion to the breed. After Richard Burton gave her a pair of Yorkies as a gift, she refused to allow them to be quarantined when she brought them to Britain, and instead hired a yacht and kept them aboard their floating kennel on the River Thames.

The little ratter from Yorkshire has come a long, long way.

The Modern Legend

Legend has it that when God had modelled all the other breeds of dog, he finally came to the Boxer. 'This,' he said, 'will be the most beautiful dog in the world.' His creation was a masterpiece. But the impetuous Boxer could not wait to see what it looked like. Before the clay could dry, it charged headlong into the nearest mirror and its nose was squashed flat.

In reality, however, the Boxer is a breed created quite recently by a German doctor. The credit for its development belongs to a Dr Toenniessen, who lived in Munich in the late nineteenth century. Continental breeders already had a strain of dog called Boxls, and by crossing one with an English Bulldog named Tom, Toenniessen saw the first long-legged Boxers born. Today the breed is so popular that it is among the top ten in the United States, Britain and Germany.

The key to its popularity undoubtedly lies in

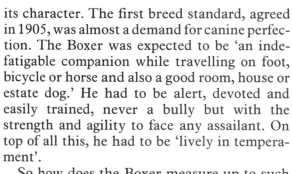

its character. The first breed standard, agreed in 1905, was almost a demand for canine perfection. The Boxer was expected to be 'an indefatigable companion while travelling on foot, bicycle or horse and also a good room, house or estate dog.' He had to be alert, devoted and easily trained, never a bully but with the strength and agility to face any assailant. On top of all this, he had to be 'lively in temperament'.

So how does the Boxer measure up to such expectations? Jo Royle had some doubts when she encountered her first examples in India. What she wanted was a guard dog. What she got was the runt of a litter of Boxers, a bitch which initially disappointed her. Although its lines and appearance were attractive, the pup showed little common sense. It was only when Jo read that the Boxer was slow to anger and had a power of discrimination that she realized she had a 'thinking dog'.

Today Jo is a top breeder of Boxers, and also shows and judges them. She believes the ideal way to treat them is as companions rather than simply as dogs. If they seem stupid or slow, it is merely because they take a while to make up their own minds.

'They won't rush in to bite you,' she says. 'They'll think about it first.'

At a deeper level, Jo clearly loves and respects the breed. She sees the Boxer as an ideal family pet, easily justifying its popularity and quick to adapt to domestic life. Adult Boxers are fastidious about keeping themselves and their environment clean. Jo speaks of one household where the owners found their Boxer walking round the pram with a haughty nose in the air when the baby's nappy needed to be changed. The Boxer's instinct to protect is equally remarkable, if we are to believe their admiring owners. They have been reported to position themselves at the top of stairs to stop babies from falling down. If a fire is left unguarded, they take their own precautions. One dog, it is claimed, dragged carpets and furniture away from an open hearth when it was left alone, and another even tapped out a burning cigarette with its paws!

Companionable as they are, it is as well to remember that the Boxer still carries in its genes the instinct to protect its family at all costs. If you visit a Boxer's home, the dog will invariably give you a wagging welcome with its stumpy tail and gently fuss you while the owner is around. If the owner leaves the room, it stands guard, watching you carefully. You are on trust until the owner signals you may go. There have even been cases of burglars being surprised by the friendliness of the Boxers left on guard. Once they tried to leave, however, they faced a different prospect. The animals stood resolutely in the way until help arrived – from the police.

Perhaps it is not surprising that so many Boxers' owners seem to have such an affinity with their animals. As one lady told us at the Ayr dog show, they are a demanding breed with a great deal of character: 'They'll do something for you the first time because they love you. They'll maybe do it the second time. But I'll tell you this, the third time's a big No!' Since she

A handshake for Sarah from Boxer 'Sting'

was competing with her dog in obedience trials, she was facing a dilemma: 'Tracking, agility and anything that's non-boring – they're super. But obedience? Hopeless.' For all that, dog and mistress were happily hugging each other at the time.

The Animals Roadshow Production Team

Executive Producer
David Martin

Producer
Ian Christie

Assistant Producers
Kate Kinninmont
Gary Hunter

Researchers
Fiona Couper
Polly Phillips

Production Manager
Murray Peterson

Production Team
Mari Hamilton
Nick Jones
Lindsay Grant
Neen MacKay
Jane Kennedy

Engineering Managers
Bryce Lamont
Bob Hood

Cameras
Harry Barclay
Stan Bradley
Dennis Callan
Brian Jobson
Gordon Penfold
Ian Turner

Vision
Dave Wood
John McMillan
Gary Fyfe

Sound
Ron Allan
Norman Canlin
Bob Gillies
John Gardner
Stuart Stevenson
Jim Young

Video Tape Editor
Peter Hayes

Stills Photographer
Tom Howatt

List of Animals Mentioned